Cromosys Publication
Your talents will not help you succeed without your skill of using them.
NIRANJAN JHA SHOWMAN
AF428897
BE MILLIONAIRE LIKE ME

Founder - Niranjan Jha Showman

Education and Technology Research Center

Patankar Park, Nallasopara (W), Mumbai. +91-9561450045

Education, Technology, Publication, Healthcare, Newsmedia, Realtor, Filmmaking

www.facebook.com/cromosys

+91-9561450045
Learn Advanced Skills
And Get Job Instantly
GERMAN
Python
FRENCH
C++
SPANISH
Java
ENGLISH
HTML5
RUSSIAN
CSS
JavaScript
Cromosys
Education and Technology Research Center
Nallasopara (W), Mumbai

Learn Web Programming
Demo-Class Free
HTML
CSS
React
JavaScript
Typescript
Bootstrap
Cromosys
20 Years of Experience
Nallasopara (W), Mumbai
+91-9561450045

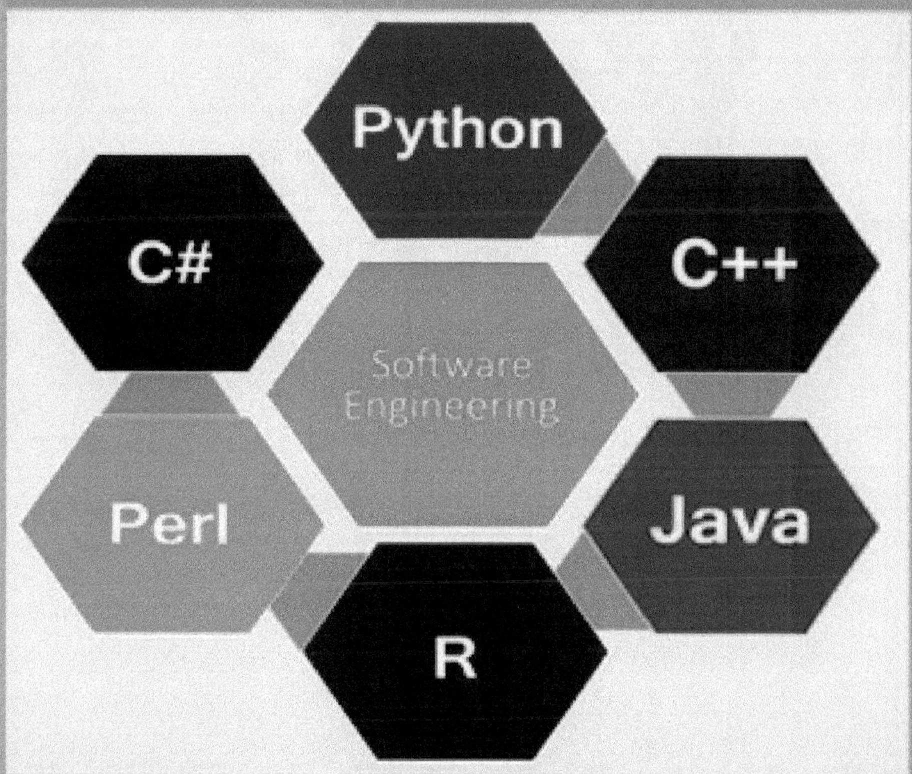

+91-9561450045
Learn Software Engineering
Demo-Class Free
Python
C#
C++
Software
Engineering
Perl
Java
R
Cromosys
20 Years of Experience
Nallasopara (W), Mumbai
+91-9561450045

25 Years of Experience
Learn Visual Multimedia

Animation VFX
Movie Editing
Game Development

Cromosys
+91-9561450045
Education and Technology Research Center
Nallasopara (W), Mumbai
www.facebook.com/cromosys

Jobs Available
For Candidates Who Know

German
French
Spanish

Vacancy in Germany, France, Spain

For Hospitality, Engineering, IT Sector
With Free Visa, Airfare and Accommodation

Cromosys
Education and Technology Research Centre
Nallasopara (W), Mumbai
+91-9561450045
20 Years of Experience

+91-9561450045
Foreign Languages Institute
German, French, Spanish
Basic and Advanced - All Levels
3 x 6 = 18 Courses
FRANCHISE
Business Offer
Teaching Materials Provided
We have 1 Million Students Globally
Great Income Assured
Global Exposure
Cromosys
20 Years of Experience
Nallasopara (W), Mumbai
+91-9561450045

Cromosys Publication

Be Millionaire Like Me

Niranjan Jha Showman

"Your talents will not help you succeed without your skill of using them."
~Niranjan Jha Showman

Preface

Cromosys Publication's "Be Millionaire Like Me" book is an ultimate motivational book. The reason to call it ultimate is that this book is written as a practical guide by the author Niranjan Jha Showman who defeated misfortune in his real life. More than an author and a motivator, he is self-motivated and a practical man who came from rags to riches. If you know people who were born in extreme poverty but became after hard work, Niranjan Jha Showman is one among them. He is called the man of Midas-touch knowing how to turn the table and hit bull's eye. The purpose of this book is to help you grow in life and achieve success no matter what bad circumstances you were born in. Amid challenges, sometimes conventional education fails to help human being achieve success. Therefore, before the life drifts away, one needs motivation to fight destiny, to defeat poverty, to frighten own fear, and be victorious.

As you start reading this book, you would like to ask questions whether it is possible to be a millionaire. And my answer to you is 'yes'. As I became, so you can also be. You can also be a millionaire after reading this book as I became. As I improved my knowledge, strength and wisdom to obviate poverty I was born in, I will teach you the same methods through this book. Till now, you may have read many motivational books, and you may have been taught motivations by many preachers. But you never know whether your motivators were self-motivated with real-life experiences. Or they were clever enough to sell their books only? Some of them may have taught you how to come out of poverty which they never experienced in their lives. They never felt how obstinate poverty is and how much hard work you need to do to come out. But with me. the story is just opposite. Since birth, up to fifteen years, I lived a disgraceful life. And after fighting all odds, turning all stones, I got success. So I got enabled to write this book. That is why this is book is the best choice of millions of readers who really want victory in life defeating problems.

It is a great achievement for any man to perform extraordinary acts, but it is even more when this is done despite terrible circumstances. The thing that makes this book stand-alone and a must-read is that, you will find my own self-applied modes of jumping out of the grave of misfortune. As you also want success, so build in your mind a perfect scene of whatever you want to accomplish. Put a lot of detail, colour, sound, scents and life into these mental scenes. Repeat them often, with faith and attention, and your subconscious mind will accept them as real experiences, and would therefore, assist you in aligning them with your reality in a most natural way. It will make any necessary changes to make your reality fit your mental images. I don't call it a book but a commandment to the international human society willing to achieve success. Some of the greatest people of the world, often regarded as the smartest minds of our century, they often had to face great obstacles, the ridicules, but ultimately they succeeded. If you get to know about their lives, you will find that they also had to learn, practice and apply some to success. The same skills that they learnt and applied, I am mentioning in this book and I believe in the fact that your life will also be brightened with fabulous colours.

Let's try to understand what success is and why you want it. Success is the state or condition of meeting a defined range of expectations. It may be viewed as the opposite of failure. The criteria for success depend on context, and may be relative to a particular observer or belief system. Being successful means the achievement of desired visions and planned goals. Furthermore, success can be a certain social status that describes a prosperous person that could also have gained fame for its favourable outcome. One of the most important key steps to achieve success in life is to know the meaning of success for your personal life. The dictionary describes success in literal sense as the following: "attaining wealth, prosperity and/or fame". And in behavioural sense, success is all about accomplishment. The accomplishment can be seen as the process to become successful and with every accomplished goal you take a step towards prosperity and a life full of success.

Cromosys, our education and technology research center, which is a path-breaking pioneer training institute for Spoken English, Foreign Languages, and Computer Science, is committed to enlightening human mind with educational endeavours, and we are doing the same from last successful twenty years. Having been teaching English and foreign languages from several years, I have come across numerous unique rules which I have elaborated and explained in this book. I believe I have done all that I could to make this book useful to you, and not only hopeful but I am sure that your success is in your hand now because this book will take you miles ahead in your expectation. We always respect the views and comments of readers, so for any communication with regards to assistance, enquiry or collaboration, we are always at your reach as it helps us improve our ability.

Niranjan Jha Showman
Trainer, Author Physician, Entrepreneur, Filmmaker, Activist
Founder - Cromosys Corporation
facebook.com/cromosys
+91-9561450045
cromosys@yahoo.com
Nallasopara (W), Mumbai, India

My other books: -
Teach Yourself German
Teach Yourself French
Teach Yourself Spanish
Teach Yourself HTML5
Teach Yourself 3ds Max
Teach Yourself Autodesk Maya
Teach Yourself C++ Programming
Teach Yourself Python Programming
Teach Yourself Java Programming
English Word Power
English Voice Accent and Pronunciation

Cromosys Corporation
Education and Technology Research Center
Education, Technology, Publication, Healthcare, Realtor, Filmmaking
facebook.com/cromosys
+91-9561450045
cromosys@yahoo.com
Nallasopara (W), Mumbai, India

About the Author

Niranjan Jha Showman
Trainer, Author, Physician, Entrepreneur, Filmmaker, Activist

Niranjan Jha Showman is a Language Scientist and Technical Researcher. He is the Award Winning author of more than fifty educational and fictional books at Amazon. He is one of the great-grandsons of the first President of India Dr. Rajendra Prasad (from adoption). He is a Public Figure, and the globally - renowned Languages Trainer of French, Spanish, and German from past twenty years. Niranjan Jha Showman is an Entrepreneur and also works as a Filmmaker in India. Being the founder and owner of Cromosys Corporation - a company located in Mumbai, India, his company is excelling in the fields of Education, Technology, Publication, Newsmedia, Realtors, Banking, and Cinemascope from past fifteen years.

Niranjan Jha Showman's good-seller educational books and novels are appreciated worldwide. He has more than one million eBook buyers online, and more than one million learners are connected to him globally. Some of his novels is critically acclaimed. He is the trainer of French, Spanish, German, English Voice and Accent, and Advanced Computer Education. He is also a political activist and the founder of Vikaswadi Party in India.

Niranjan Jha Showman is the man who came from rags to riches, he who knows how to turn the table, and he, whom you call the man of Midas-touch, and Renaissance man. He has observed lives from the Pandora of monkeys to the sanctuary of monks, not only down-to-earth but down-to-grave. He is a B. Com. graduate, and B. Ed. from Delhi University, and diploma holder in French, Spanish and German from America. You can watch his songs, movies, educational videos and many more things by typing "Niranjan Jha Showman" in Google.

Niranjan Jha Showman
+91-9561450045
cromosys@yahoo.com
Nallasopara (W), Mumbai, India
www.facebook.com/cromosys
www.notionpress.com/author/814619
www.facebook.com/niranjanshowman
www.facebook.com/vikaswadiparty

Statutory
This book with its content is the registered property of the author Niranjan Jha Showman.
The author and his Cromosys Publication holds all necessary rights of this book.
The copyright certificate of this book is attached at the end of this book.

This book is a copyright and its content is the registered property of the author Niranjan Jha Showman. The author and his Cromosys Publication holds all necessary rights of this book. All the writing works that include all the educational, non-educational books, novels, and articles of the writer Niranjan Jha Showman, are the registered content under MAHENG12112/13/1/2009-TC and the endorsement no. 3244 28/5/2009 with the Ministry of Information and Broadcasting, Govt. of India. Any plagiarism in this regard will attract strict legal action. Any further publication or production of any of his books requires his written permission. The copyright certificate of this book is attached at the end of this book.

Chapter 1

Positive Thinking

The first step of positive thinking is to believe in oneself. You have to create a belief in your mind that you are born to get success in your life. And the success that you want, for that, you should have a mission. Remember that the generation after generation, human race suffered a lot because of the dearth of belief. Most of the people have a mindset that they are born by the grace of some supernatural power, and so everything will be set automatically for their comfort. What they forget is that their birth is a result of a natural phenomenon, so only their deeds will create the destination of their lives, and not any supernatural power.

Human birth is not a beneficence!

It is not a blessing that its all needs will be automatically fulfilled. In nature, the biological incidents beget life. So after you are born, it's your duty to work for your need. And it is your wisdom that helps you lead a comfortable life. And in the earth, when population increases, as it keeps increasing, it generates competition in which you're required to work hard… even harder. Remember that you are not blessed or bound with destiny. In this infinite world, you have your own freedom. Therefore, you are absolutely free to run or ruin your life.

Challenges in Life

Beethoven is widely regarded as one of the greatest composers. He gave his first public performance as a pianist at the age of eight. He studied in Vienna under the guidance of Mozart. By his mid-twenties he had earned a name for himself as a great pianist known for unpredictable and brilliant improvisations. In the year 1796, he began losing his hearing. In spite of his illness, he immersed himself in his work and created some of the greatest works of music. The pianist's finest works are also the finest works of their kind in music history: the 9th Symphony, the 5th Piano Concerto, the Violin Concerto, the Late Quartets, and his Missa Solemnis. He achieved all this despite being completely deaf for the last twenty five years of his life.

Sudha Chandran was born in a Tamil family of Chennai, South India. She completed her Masters in Economics from Mumbai. On one of her return trips from Mumbai to Chennai, she met with an accident resulting in the amputation of her right leg. She was given an artificial leg. Despite this terrible disability, she became one of the most accomplished and acclaimed dancers of the Indian subcontinent. She has received and still receives invitations to perform all over the world. She has been honoured with numerous awards and has performed all over the world. She appears often on television and in films.

"Not taking risk in life is the biggest risk." – Shiv Khera

Life brings challenges for many people, but victorious are those who defeat setbacks and make their own path of success. Men are not born with circumstances but create them. Don't sit idle and let darkness cover you. Don't laze and let adversity arrest you. Never underrate yourself and let depression attack you. Don't wait for things to happen but make them happen.

Stephen William Hawking is a British theoretical physicist, whose scientific career spans over forty years. His books and public appearances have made him an academic celebrity and he is an honorary fellow of the Royal Society of Arts, a lifetime member of the Pontifical Academy of Sciences, and in 2009 was awarded the Presidential Medal of Freedom, the highest civilian award in the United States. Stephen Hawking is severely disabled by motor neuron disease, likely a variant of the disease known as amyotrophic lateral sclerosis or ALS.

Symptoms of the disorder first appeared while he was enrolled at Cambridge. He lost his balance and fell down a flight of stairs, hitting his head. Worried that he would lose his genius, he took the Mensa test to verify that his intellectual abilities were intact. The diagnosis of motor neuron disease came when Hawking was twenty one, shortly before his first marriage. The doctors said he would not survive more than two or three years. Hawking gradually lost the use of his arms, legs, and voice, and as of 2009 was completely paralyzed. But gradually he started recovering and because of his belief to make life worthwhile his deeds reached him to the destination.

All these facts may not feel factual to you if you have a negative attitude. As you are reading this book, little by little, create some thoughts in your mind of making your life also good. Imagine how good it will be if you elevate your life higher than where it is. Remember that there are no great people in this world, only great challenges which ordinary people rise to meet. And in order to succeed, your desire for success should be greater than your fear for failure. Every adversity has within it the seeds of an equivalent or a greater benefit as you meet the circumstances of life they may seem adverse and damaging. Later you find that every so-called misfortune sows the seed of greater fortune to come. To help this mighty dynamic work its wonders in your life, close the door on your past. Carry along with you only what is pleasant and instructive. Leaving gloom and pain behind you, you can see the future and make it yours.

Go Extra Mile

The mind of man is far more wonderful than any machine. Within it, however, there seems to be a kind of Yes-No valve at the focal point of thinking. It is as though your awareness of a circumstance of life-sent to your brain by your sight, hearing and other senses-presents itself at the Yes-No point to be processed. A person who maintains a positive attitude will find every possible Yes in that circumstance and make it part of his life. A person who maintains a negative mental attitude will lean toward the No side, miss much that is good, live with much that is painful and damaging.

"Winners are those who keep breaking their own records." – Niranjan Jha Showman

In work situations especially, grudges and a feeling of resentment play havoc with the mind's ability to conceive and achieve. Going the extra mile has a tonic effect in relieving the mind of built-in obstacles. Add to your work more than you are paid for. Always qualify yourself for the next step upward and the steps beyond. People who succeed are not people who hold grudges or who with- hold their best work, but those who in every act and thought pave their way toward greater things.

Here is a story that teaches us not to follow things blindly.

Story – The Old Clock

There was a roadside clock shop in London. Every morning and evening people passed through the way. One day an old man comes in front of the shop, he stops for a minute, does something and goes away. As it is the first day, so the shopkeeper doesn't notice. The next day again the old man comes and does the same. By the time the shopkeeper wants to talk, the man is already gone. So the next day, the shopkeeper comes out and starts waiting for him.

When he comes, he asks, "Uncle, I'm the owner of this shop. I see that you do here something every day. May I know what you do?" The uncle says, "My son, I work as a security guard for this nearby company. My job is to blow siren at 5 pm. Then the labors go home. But as I am old, my watch is also old, and loses time every night. So I look at your big clock and set the time of my watch." Hearing this, the shopkeeper starts laughing. The uncle asks, "I told you the truth, now why are you laughing?" The shopkeeper says, "Uncle, this big clock is also very old and loses time every day. So when I hear your siren at 5 pm, I set the time of this clock every day.

<u>How Belief Works?</u>

If you believe that you can also bring changes in your life, apply your skills with patience. You never learn from problems, but you learn from the way you solve them. And, as you are living in a competitive world, people would know you by what you are best at, not what you are mediocre at. You need to get or develop ideas to solve your problems. And while solving problems, you have to stand strong because there comes challenges while fighting odds. Here you can get some real and positive ideas from the life of great personalities mentioned below. Sam Walton, who is a big-box retailing behemoth, the idea for Walmart came from the mind of this unassuming farm boy from Oklahoma. Walton spent his early years living on his family's farm, and then moved to Missouri when his father decided to become a farm loan appraiser.

"The pessimist sees difficulty in every opportunity. The optimist sees opportunity in every difficulty." – Winston Churchill

Sam showed great ambition from an early age; he became Missouri's youngest ever Eagle Scout when he received that award in 8th grade, and he was elected class president his senior year in high school. Despite growing up during the Great Depression and working odd jobs like delivering newspapers to help support his family, he excelled academically throughout his school years. He paid his way through the University of Missouri by working as a lifeguard, newspaper delivery boy, and waiter. When he graduated, he took jobs at JC Penney's and at a DuPont's munitions plant before serving in the army during World War Second.

After the war, Walton was determined to open his own variety store. He pooled the substantial amount of money he saved while in the military and with a loan from his father-in-law, bought a Ben Franklin store in Newport, Arkansas. Walton supplied customers with a wide variety of goods at low prices and kept those prices low by buying in high volume directly from wholesalers. The store was highly successful, and Walton then opened his own store, "Walton's Five & Dime" in Bentonville. In 1962, Walton introduced the first true Wal-Mart to Rogers, AR. That store, like all his others, turned a nice profit, and Walton began to expand the franchise across the country, making it the world's largest retailer by 1991. He reigned as America's richest man from 1985-1988, and were he alive today, he would be the world's richest man, with wealth double that of Bill Gates. Very few people know that Walmart lost their first store because they didn't own the land their store was built on.

Keep yourself aware of life's endless combinations of circumstances. Do not believe that one experience of lost love or lost opportunity or other misfortune has ended your chances of winning what you thought you had lost. Some of the world's greatest men knew failure after failure as they grew toward their ultimate success.

If you also want to be successful, create these habits in yourself:

- Read good books.
- Meet good people.
- Dream something big.
- Learn and keep learning.
- Start your venture.
- Work hard and sustain.

Nothing but a mental attitude? Nothing but a mental attitude, but it is right there that your success or your failure, your peace of mind or your nervous tension, your tendency toward good health or your tendency toward illness begins. Fortunately it is possible for anyone to make the change from negativism to positivism, and thus basically condition his brain to bring all that is good in life.

"Do not go where the path may lead, go instead where there is no path and leave a trail." – Ralph Waldo Emerson

Mind Your Mind

When you speak of failure you attract failure, when you speak of success you attract success. Mind doesn't attract good things automatically. We need to force our mind to run in the right direction. One's difficult upbringing and bothering circumstances affect their mind. And when the mind is affected, there are chances that it won't work in the right direction. You need to watch your mind before minding our mission.

The symptoms of negative minds are as follows:

1. Unable to think properly.
2. Unwilling to accept challenges.
3. Disbelief towards ambition.
4. Making castle in air.
5. Faltering and scattering.
6. Unable to learn new things.
7. Creating physical abnormality during challenges.
8. Generating fear over desire of success.
9. Causing depression.

Ways to cure negative minds:

A. Identity yourself.
B. Soothe your mind to vent out negativity.
C. Apply medication if needed.
D. Give right food to body.
E. Take proper sleep in night.
F. Abstain from intoxication.
G. Examine your behaviour.
H. Furnish your ambition.
I. Work hard and stay happy.

Control your mental attitude with definiteness of purpose. Emerson said: 'The world makes way for a man who knows where he is going." Think what it means to know where you are going! Automatically you rid yourself of all kinds of fears and doubts which may have crept into the making-up-your-mind pro- cess. Your purpose is definite and-presto!-all the limitless forces of your mind focus upon that purpose and no other. Knowing your purpose, you cannot be led astray by circumstances or words which have nothing to do with your purpose. Where, before, a day's work may have contained a good deal of wasted motion, now your efforts are lined up so that each mental or physical motion helps every other motion.

"Do one thing every day that scares you." – Eleanor Roosevelt

Story – Afternoon Darkness

There was a writer in London and one day he was taking a morning walk on the hills. Suddenly a storm comes and he falls down. While rolling down, he comes into the valley, and loses the direction to go back home. At some distance into the valley, he only sees some huts. As the writer gets in, he sees an old man sitting inside. He says: Sir, I am from the city and I fell down here because of the storm. Could you tell me how to go back to my house? The old man says: City… House… I haven't heard these words before. Perhaps you are dreaming, so you can go to sleep. But the old man's daughter was listening, so she says to her father: Perhaps this stranger is saying something true. Can we help him in any manner?

The old man replies: Yes, we'll take him to our doctor. As they come out, the writer notices that it was a hamlet of all blind people, so the doctor was also blind. Upon reaching the doctor, the old man says: This stranger came to me this morning looking for his city and house. As I don't know anything about it, so can you please check what the problem with him is? The doctor examine his body and replies: Uncle, I find two organs above his nose and below forehead. If I remove them, he will be like us and will not talk anything irrelevant. Hearing this, the writer takes his steps back and starts running. In fear, he crosses two hills, and then sits down with closed eyes because of tiredness. When he opens eyes, he sees his own city… his own house.

Power of Attraction

Arnold Schwarzenegger, who is a famous actor-turned-governor of California, made the improbable leap from bodybuilder and actor to politician. Arnold Schwarzenegger was born in a small village in Austria. His cold and abusive father was the local police chief, and yet money was always tight for the family. Life in the unhappy household left Arnold determined to leave home and find fame and fortune. Deciding at an early age to make bodybuilding a career, Schwarzenegger started pumping iron at age 14. He also studied psychology to better sharpen his mind's strength and willpower.

Nothing could keep Schwarzenegger from his love of bodybuilding. As a youth he busted into the gym when it was closed on weekends and as a soldier he went AWOL to enter a competition. Years of sweat and toil paid off when Arnold, at age 20, became the youngest ever winner of the Mr. Universe competition, a title he would win four more times. He continued training while simultaneously attending business school and working at a gym. At age 21, he moved to America to become a star of the silver screen. He continued to compete in bodybuilding and won the Mr. Olympia title seven times. Arnold's entrance into film was far more difficult than his workouts. With a thick accent and bulking body, he met many rejections before finally landing roles.

"You see things and say: why? I dream non-existing thing and say: why not?" – Bernard

After becoming a blockbuster action-star, Schwarzenegger's next obstacle to conquer was politics. In 2003, overcoming his inexperience, accent, and having appeared in as Mr. Freeze in Batman and Robin, Arnold won the California recall election and became the governor of California. And now the entire world knows the fame of Arnold Schwarzenegger whether in movies or American politics.

Walt Disney experienced a less than idyllic childhood. Before he dominated the cartoon and amusement-park empire, he worked as an ambulance driver in France during World War I. He took the gig after he was rejected from the army for being underage. And once, he was fired from a newspaper for lacking imagination and having no original ideas. His father wandered from one job to another looking to find success, and often needing to rely on his brother to stay afloat. Walt lacked not just financial security, but for affection; his father was an abusive man. Walt was determined to blaze his own path of success and not end up like his dad. At age 16, he dropped out of high school and served in the ambulance corps during World War I. After the war, Disney found work creating ads for businesses in Kansas City. He was fascinated by the emerging field of animation and decided to set up his own animation business. Unable yet to manage money effectively, the business went bankrupt.

Then Disney set up a studio in Hollywood and began turning out cartoons, culminating in the enormously popular Steamboat Willie in 1928. Over the next several years, Disney introduced equally beloved characters such as Donald Duck, Goofy, and Pluto. In 1934, Disney began to work on his most ambitious idea yet: a full-length animated feature. Dubbed "Disney's folly" by his critics, most thought the idea would spell the demise of the Disney studio. Instead, Snow White and the Seven Dwarves was a smashing success. The film was followed by a myriad of other beloved full-length features and animated shorts. In the 1950's Disney expanded the work of his company to include the production of live-action films. Disney also completed an ambitious project few believed could be a success: the 1955 opening of Disneyland. Disneyworld followed in 1964 and now we all know about its fame.

Sufficient money is necessary to almost everyone who wishes to attain peace of mind, but wealth can steal happiness away from those who make it dishonestly or do not use it correctly. Use your work and your wealth to help others. Above all, make sure that as you climb the ladder of success you do not step upon anyone else. Moreover, there are certain "control levers" which the Creator makes available to us, and it is easy to see how successful people use these levers, once you know what they are. I shall give you some here and some in other chapters so as to reinforce your memory. Now and then you will find repetition of names, facts and methods in this books, always with a view toward helping you remember.

You can see the connection with building wealth, for work done well is a basic wealth-builder. Now see the connection with peace of mind. A man who works wholeheartedly at his job is not concerned with such matters as finding fault with others, disturbing his conscience by cutting comers in his work, watching the clock and so forth.

"It is better to light a candle than to curse the darkness." – Columbus

Power of Teaching

Socrates taught Plato:
'Life is beautiful, live like a seeker.'

Plato taught Aristotle:
'Life is beautiful, live like an achiever.'

Aristotle taught Alexander:
'Life is beautiful, live like a conqueror.'

Alexander taught himself:
'Life is beautiful only if I become a conqueror.'

There is a story that truly depicts power of teaching. Somewhere in 1794, Napoleon Bonaparte was caught by one of his rival kings in France. He was put in cell where he felt very boring to pass time. He told the rival king to send him a few people whom he would teach war strategy. He got a small group of ordinary men to be taught. They were ordinary but loyal to the king. But in ten days, he induced their mind in such a way that with their help Napoleon came out of the cell and attacked the king. Finally Napoleon defeated the king. This story is known as the best example of the power of teaching.

Dell Corporation

Dell Corporation was established in 1984 in the USA.
The founder of this company is Michael Dell.
He was born in 1965 in the state of Texas.
He worked first at a Chinese restaurant to earn money.
Then he started the business of upgrading computers.
In 1984 Michael registered his company as PC's Limited.
Same year, he changed it to Dell Corporation.
Dell ranked top 500 companies of the world.
It started earning great by selling computers on web.
He has worked as an advisor of the US President's Council.
He resides at Austin in Texas with wife and three children.
Dell's net worth is estimated $ 15 billion.

"If you win, you need not explain. But if you lose, you shouldn't be there to explain." – Hitler

Chapter 2

The Surprising Facts

Everybody started somewhere! In fact, people who have achieved fame and fortune often had very small beginnings. They started working with limited resources. You can check out the first jobs of these well-known names. Nicolas Cage used to sell popcorn at the Fairfax Theatre. Lady Gaga used to work as a waitress at a restaurant in New York. Brad Pitt used to work for El Pollo Loco restaurant on Sunset Boulevard often dressing up in a chicken costume! Tom Hanks used to be a popcorn and peanuts vendor. Harrison Ford still enjoys carpentry. He was a self-taught carpenter who made cabinets for George Lucas. It was his cabinet-making job that landed him a tiny role in Lucas' American Graffiti. Rest is history. Sandra Bullock used to work as a bartender while in college. Marlon Brando was a high school dropout. He even worked as a ditch digger among many other jobs in his youth.

Sharon Stone and Rachel McAdams had worked with Mc Donald's when they were young. Hollywood's handsome hunk George Clooney used to sell suits, worked in department store, and even in construction sites. Captain Jack Sparrow used to sell ballpoint pens in his early life! Tom Cruise wanted to become a catholic priest and he even joined a Franciscan seminary! He would have become a hunky priest, but God had different plans! Megan Fox, in her teens, worked for a shop. Pamela Anderson used to be a fitness instructor before. Bon Jovi's first job was making Christmas decorations. Singer Sting worked as a bus conductor, construction labourer, tax officer and teacher before becoming a successful musician.

Let's look into the life of Sylvester Stallone. Sylvester's life was harder than Rocky Balboa's. He used to work as a lion cage cleaner at Central Park Zoo. After finding himself homeless, Stallone had to no other way but to act in a porn flick for a mere $ 200. Al Pacino and Quentin Tarantino used to work as cinema ushers. Pop diva Madonna survived on her dreams and the meagre income she used to get from a job at 'Dunkin' Donuts' when she arrived in 'Big Apple'.

I believe these people overcame every single shortcoming by the sheer passion. I don't know if you're born with this kind of passion, or if you can learn it. But I do know you need it. The meaning of life is not simply to exist, to survive, but to move ahead, to go up, to achieve, to conquer. The way to get started is to quit talking and begin doing.

I have mentioned that many eminently successful men do not possess any greater intelli- gence than most other men possess. Yet their achievements are such that we may say that these men have "genius." Surely it is the positive mental attitude of these men which makes their brain-power, not greater, but more efficient and more available than most others'. When I spoke to such men as Henry Ford, Andrew Carnegie and Thomas A. Edison, I spoke with minds free of any fear or doubt that they could do anything they wished to do.

"To live is to have problems, and to solve problems is to grow intellectually." – Tom Wujec

Dealing With Stress?

It is true that when you start working hard on your mission, it increases your level of stress. And stress is one of biggest reasons people quit working. You need to understand that every toiler doesn't succeed but every successful person has to be a toiler. Here I need to mentions some reasons why some people quit before achieving the target?

Look at the reasons of quitting:

- Choose a wrong goal.
- Fail to manage stress.
- Doesn't give good food to body.
- Doesn't drink enough water.
- Ignore physical problem.
- Fail to keep oneself happy.
- Distance from good friends.
- No addition to motivation.
- Sexual frustration.

Ways of sustainability:

- Work hard but also laugh large.
- Develop friend circle.
- Go for exercise regularly.
- Find your liking and fulfil.
- Consume limited amount of liquor if needed.
- Ask your doctor in physical discomfort.
- Attach with music, sports and movies.
- Spend time with loved ones.
- Antidepressant treatment in severe stress.

<u>**You Are Unique**</u>

Think what a remarkable, un-duplicable, and miraculous thing it is to be you! As God gave birth to you, so you are a born winner, otherwise you would have been dead as a sperm in your father's semen. Remember that you are victorious. Of all the people who have come and gone on the earth, since the beginning of time, not one of them is like you! No one who has ever lived or is to come has had your combination of abilities, talents, appearance, friends, acquaintances, burdens, sorrows and opportunities.

"Some people change themselves as per the frame of time. Some people make the frame itself changed." – Arabic proverb.

No one's hair grows exactly the way yours does. No one's finger prints are like yours. No one has the same combination of secret inside jokes and family expressions that you know. The few people who laugh at all the same things you do, they don't sneeze the way you do. No one prays about exactly the same concerns as you do. No one is loved by the same combination of people that love you. No one before, no one to come, you are absolute unique.

Enjoy that uniqueness. You do not have to pretend in order to seem more like someone else. You weren't meant to be like someone else. You were meant to be different. Nowhere ever in all of history will the same things be going on in anyone's mind, soul and spirit as are going on in yours right now. If you did not exist, there would be a hole in creation, a gap in history, something missing from the plan for humankind. Treasure your uniqueness. It is a gift given only to you. Enjoy it and share it! You must experience and accept the extremes, because if the contrast is lost, you lose the value of everything. Your vision should be clear and strong because it your vision that leads you and its strength keep you positive in your difficult time. Your truest life is when you are in your dream awake! Happiness comes in life by doing good works, and you do good works when you are happy in life. Be cheerful and remain cheerful!

No one can reach out to others in the same way that you can. No one can speak your words. No one can convey your meanings. No one can comfort with your kind of comfort. No one can bring your kind of understanding to another person. No one can be cheerful and light-hearted and joyous in your way. No one can smile your smile. No one else can bring the whole unique impact of you to another human being. Share your uniqueness. Let it be free to flow out among your family and friends and people you meet in the rush and clutter of living wherever you are. That gift of yourself was given you to enjoy and share. Give yourself away! See it! Receive it! Let it tickle you! Let it inform you and nudge you and inspire you! You are unique!

Story – Keep the Fire Burning

A crew of Discovery channel enters a forest in Mexico. As they go deep inside, they observe something unusual. They see some smokes coming from somewhere as it appeared man-made and not natural. Following the direction of the smoke and ready with video-shooting, they reach the exact spot. Now they see some tribal sitting in a circle around the fire. They were putting coals in fire to keep it burning.

After great efforts, the crew members succeed in asking them reason of sitting there. They said in their language that their ancestors had invented fire. But the next generation forgot to create fire. So they found some fire at some place, brought them here, and they sit to guard the fire and keep it burning since ages. And they have no hope of fire being found anywhere else. Feeling perplexed, the crew members bring some of the tribal out of forest. The jungly people, after coming out feel astonished seeing how much humans have done with fire in new world!

"You'll never have a significant success until it's an obsession for you." – Niranjan Jha Showman

How Should Be Your Goal?

While choosing your goal for life you need to take care for certain things. Never imitate the goal of other because you may not have the X factor for that particular field. As most of the youngsters want to be a movie actor, but that is not their right goal. One who has some inbuilt character, quality and deservance will become actor. Ask yourself what you like, what to go for and what you devote to. That is where your goal is. Here I mention are some tips to understand and choose your right goal:

1. Choose goal of your interest.
2. Make sure it is not obsolete.
3. Divide it in small tasks.
4. Find all available resources.
5. Give time in knowing more about it.
6. Talk to people of that field.
7. Invest money when required.
8. Publicize your achievement.

Goal as Obsession

The key to success is obsession. Obsession is about focus and a deep interest in the matter. When I think about this idea I make associations to my lifelong interest in art. Most people have a dream in life, a vision of who or what they'd like to be in the future. At a minimum, everyone has interests and values that determine what they want out of their lives. Even so, trying to set achievable goals that you'll work for over the course of many years can be daunting. It can be hard to know where to even begin, and the things you hope to achieve may seem impossible. But, if you're well-prepared you may be able to set goals for your life that are just as fulfilling to work toward as to achieve.

Think about what you want?

Many people have only a vague sense of what they want from life. In this first step, your task is to start converting ideas like "happiness" or "security" into things you would like to do. Get a pen and some paper and start writing down things that are important to you in life. It's okay to be general at this stage, but try not to be vague. For example, if the first thing that pops into your head is "happiness," that's fine. But try to define that term. What does "happiness" mean to you? What would you consider a happy life?

"Getting angry is easy, but getting it at right time is wisdom." – Aristotle

Write about your goal. One good way to start moving from general to specific is to do some free-writing about yourself. Think about your personality and your interests. This can help you define what is most important to you. Try writing about how you enjoy spending your time. Begin your brainstorming by writing down what you enjoy doing and what excites you. Don't limit yourself to activities or experiences that you think are productive or "worth doing." The point of brainstorming is to get down as many ideas as possible, and this list will be useful later on in the process. Write about things you are interested in and/or would like to learn more about. Are you interested in science? In literature? In music? Any of these could become lifelong pursuits.

Write about things about yourself you'd like to improve. Are you hoping to develop your skills as a public speaker? As a writer? As a photographer? Again, these can all become life-long pursuits. Imagine your future. Think about your ideal future. What does it look like? Ask yourself questions that will help you get to a detailed picture. Make your goals specific. After all this brainstorming, you should have some ideas about what you'd like to do with your life. In fact, you probably have several! Now is the time to make them as specific as possible. Think about why you want to achieve something. By now, you probably have a few strong contenders for life goals. Examine each one and ask yourself: "why do I want that?" Your answers may lead you to revise your goals. In general, setting goals that are meaningful to you because they relate to your personal values will make you more likely to succeed at reaching them.

True Story of a Mathematician

We need to know about a great personality from the field of teaching. This is a quite inspirational story of a man of Bihar (India). Anand kumar is a mathematician in Patna city of India. He developed an indomitable affection and love towards mathematics and possesses exceptional mathematical abilities. His role model is great Indian mathematician Ramanujan. During graduation, He submitted papers on Number Theory, which were published in Mathematical Spectrum and The Mathematical Gazette. He worked hard and dreamed of getting into one of the world's best university Cambridge. And one day he got admission to Cambridge. But very soon he realized that his father cannot afford his educational expenses at Cambridge. He and his father searched helplessly for a sponsor all over India but nobody came up. And one day his family's only breadwinner: his father died and his last hope of getting good education diminished. He gave up the dream of Cambridge and came back to his home in Patna, Bihar.

He would work on Mathematics during day time and would sell eatables in evenings with his mother, who had started a small business from home to support her family. He also tutored students in maths to earn extra money. He rented a classroom for Rs 500 a month, and began his own institute, the Ramanujam School of Mathematics (RSM). Within a year, his class grew from two students to thirty six, and after three years there were almost 500 students enrolled. Then in early 2000, when a poor student came to him seeking coaching for IIT-JEE, who couldn't afford the annual admission fee due to poverty, Kumar was motivated to start the Super 30 program in 2003, for which he is now well-known.

"You cannot touch the sky if you are living with crabs." – Niranjan Jha Showman

Every year in August, since 2003, the Ramanujan School of Mathematics, now a trust, holds a competitive test to select 30 students for the 'Super 30' scheme. About 4,000 to 5,000 students appear at the test, and eventually he takes thirty intelligent students from economically down backward sections which included beggars, hawkers, and auto-driver's children. He tutors them, and provides study materials and lodging for a year. He prepares them for the Joint Entrance Examination for the Indian Institutes of Technology (IIT). Anand Kumar's mother, Jayanti Devi, cooks for the students studying there, and his brother Pranav Kumar takes care of the management. Out of 270 students he tutored from 2002-2011, 236 students have made an admission to IIT. All of them are from very poor background. In 2010, all the students of Super 30 cleared IIT JEE entrance.

America's President Obama read about Anand in TIME magazine and sent a special envoy to check the work done by him and offered all the assistance. Discovery Channel broadcast a one-hour-long program on Super 30, and half a page has been devoted to Kumar in The New York Times. Actress and ex-Miss Japan Norika Fujiwara visited Patna to make a documentary on Anand's initiatives. Kumar has been featured in programmes by the BBC. He has spoken about his experiences at Indian Institute of Management Ahmedabad. He is in the Limca Book of Records (2009) for his contribution in helping poor students crack IIT-JEE by providing them free coaching. He was awarded the S. Ramanujan Award of 2010 by the Institute for Research and Documentation in Social Sciences (IRDS). In April 2011, Anand Kumar was selected by Europe's magazine Focus as "one of the global personalities who have the ability to shape exceptionally talented people.

Remember, as deep your foundation is, so tall you can construct the building. If you have seen all the obstacles of life, then no one can divert you from your path of success. You can be the man of Midas touch. You can be what you want to be. Of course, emptying the mind is not enough. When the mind is emptied, something is bound to enter. The mind cannot long remain a vacuum. You cannot go around permanently with an empty mind. I admit that some people seem to accomplish that feat, but by and large it is necessary to refill the emptied mind or the old, unhappy thoughts which you have cast out will come sneaking in again.

To prevent that happening, immediately start filling your mind with creative and healthy thoughts. Then when the old fears, hates, and worries that have haunted you for so long try to edge back in, they will in effect find a sign on the door of your mind reading "occupied." They may struggle for admission, for having lived in your mind for a long time, they feel at home there. But the new and healthy thoughts which you have taken in will now be stronger and better fortified, and therefore able to repulse them. Presently the old thoughts will give up altogether and leave you alone. You will permanently enjoy a mind full of peace.

So, you decide what you want to do, dedicate yourself to your work and be determined. Remember that opportunity will not come to wake you up; you have to go to the opportunity to embrace. Keep in mind that good time will not alarm you, you need to recognize the good time and start working for your success. Once you accept that great task and set my mind confidently toward it, you'll find that your imagined obstacles simply melts away. Of course your positive mental attitude helps you not only in finding out the success secrets of some five hundred of America's wealthiest men, but also in making considerably more than a mere living.

"Money is the sixth sense. If you don't have this, you can't enjoy your five senses properly." – Swett Marden

Self-made Rich

The self-made man is he who comes from unpromising circumstances, who is not born into privilege and wealth, and yet by his own efforts, by pulling himself up by the bootstraps, manages to become a great success. The discussion of self-made men is the discussion of manhood itself in its broadest and comprehensive sense. The story of the self-made man is the story of manliness personified. The self-made man harnesses and utilizes the most important masculine qualities: hard work, perseverance, and most of all, personal responsibility. The story of the self-made man embodies the goal of every man: to become the captain of his own destiny. There are numerous of the stories of the people who were born poor but they made themselves rich. In fact, according to a survey, sixty percent of rich people of the world were poor when they were born.

You may need to ask me how it happens. I will like to tell you a secret. Some people learn a great lesson from poverty which nothing else can teach them. And the lesson is of conviction. If poverty is taken in an optimistic sense, it strengthens your will power to bear the problems of your life that would come in your way of getting success. Remember that a successful person cannot make his children automatically success until they also work hard. There are many examples of it. There are many film stars who could not make their children stars, because their children fell weak in conviction. With the power of money they may be brought to the light, but in the light they would feel ashamed seeing their hollowness.

We can learn from this short story that a man found a cocoon for a butterfly. One day a small opening appeared, he sat and watched the butterfly for several hours as it struggled to force its body through the little hole. Then it seemed to stop making any progress. It appeared as if it had gotten as far as it could and could go no farther. Then the man decided to help the butterfly. He took a pair of scissors and snipped the remaining bit of the cocoon. The butterfly then emerged easily. Something was strange. The butterfly had a swollen body and shrivelled wings. The butterfly spent the rest of its life crawling around with a swollen body and deformed wings. It was never able to fly. What the man in his kindness and haste did not understand, was that the restricting cocoon and the struggle required for the butterfly to get through the small opening of the cocoon are God`s way of forcing fluid from the body of the butterfly into its wings so that it would be ready for flight once it achieved its freedom from the cocoon. Sometimes struggles are exactly what we need in our life.

Are you aware of the general principle of radio broad- casting? It is this: when electrical vibrations of rapid frequency are impressed upon a wire, those vibrations leap into space. Another wire far away-the receiving antenna-can pick them up, and thus a message or a picture is transmitted over thousands of miles, or millions of miles in space-age communication. There are electrical currents in the brain. They give you a private broadcasting station through which you may send out any kind of thought vibrations you desire. Keep that station busy sending out thoughts of a positive nature, thoughts which will benefit others, and you will find you can receive kindred thought vibrations from other minds whose attitude is tuned to yours.

"The secret of walking on water is knowing where the stones are." – Edison

Rich People Who Were Born Poor

Ever wondered if the famous rich people you hear about a lot were whether born poor or rich? It turns out in the last century and few decades, most of the millionaires or billionaires were rather self-made. They didn't have the money and luxury they have now when they were born to their parents. Of course, some of them did get help from their parents but they add more values to the assets and properties and thus became rich. Here we won't be talking about the people who inherited wealth from their parents or ancestor. We will be discussing the rags to riches story; list of poor people who became rich. Larry Ellison is the genius person behind the success of Oracle Software Company and his wealth is close to $28 billion. He is born to a single teenage unwed mother who gave birth to him in the Bronx.

Larry never knew his father, and still an infant, he was shipped off to Chicago to be taken care of and eventually adopted by, his mother's aunt and uncle. Ellison grew up in a two bedroom apartment and attended two years of college before dropping out when his adoptive mother died. Interested in computer and software design, he went to work for Ampex Corporation. He founded a database company Oracle in 1977 with $2000 of his own money. His company is now one of the world's biggest software companies. He got $130 million pay package in 2009, making him second-highest-paid CEO in the US, according to the recent compensation survey. Greatly successful, the company made Ellison a billionaire many times over and continues to secure his place as the 9th richest man in the world.

Barack Obama's childhood was far from typical. He was born to a white mother and Kenyan father in Hawaii. His father went back to Kenya when he was only 2 and saw his son only once more. His mother married again to an Indonesian, and the family moved to Indonesia. Barack lived there for several years and then returned to Hawaii to live with his grandparents. He graduated from Columbia University, worked as a community organizer in Chicago for 3 years, and then went to Harvard Law School. While there he became the first African-American to be elected as president of the Harvard Law Review. Obama returned to Chicago and spent 12 years as a professor at the Law School of University of Chicago. He was elected to the Illinois State Senate in 1996 and the US Senate in 2004. After only one term as Senator, Obama won the presidential election and became the first black president in United States history.

J.K. Rowling is the author of Harry Potter book and movie series. She currently has $1 billion but will grow her wealth as she keeps earning royalty fees. While writing wizardry single mother lived on welfare in Edinburgh, Scotland. Broke and depressed, author once told reporters she contemplated suicide. Rowling's Harry Potter and the Sorcerer's Stone were published in 1997 and quickly became a bestseller and the first of a seven-book series that captivated children and adults worldwide. First of films series released in 2001. First six of the magical movies grossed more than $5 billion.

"Profit without risk, experience without danger and reward without hard work, is as impossible as life without being born." – Gouthey

Apple Foundation

Apple was established in a garage of San Francisco in 1976.
Its founder Steve Jobs was born in 1955 in the USA.
His father was a machinist and mother was a clerk.
Steve got educated up to intermediate.
He attended HP computer lectures at Palo Alto, California.
Later Steve was hired there on temporary basis.
He dropped out college because of money problem.
He got a technician job for Atari company.
He travelled India to know about Buddhism.
He established Apple company in his parents' garage.
Apple invented Macintosh computer operating system.
Apple's products are iPod, iTunes, and iPhones.
It has the highest brand value in the entire world.

<u>Rags to Riches</u>

Making your mark on the world is hard. If it were easy, everybody would do it. But it takes patience, it takes commitment, and it comes with plenty of failure along the way. The real test is not whether you avoid this failure, because you won't. It's whether you let it harden or shame you into inaction, or whether you learn from it; whether you choose to persevere.

Ronald Reagan, who turned his acting career into a successful presidency, certainly earns the title of self-made man. There was no silver spoon in the mouth of Ronald when he came into the world in 1911. Born in Illinois, his father was a salesman who was always looking for better work. Reagan thus grew up moving from one tiny town in Illinois to the next, often living in apartments above banks and stores. After college, he became a radio announcer and landed a film contract with Warner Brothers. After a stint in the military, Reagan became the president of the Screen Actors Guild. He began his foray into politics by working on Barry Goldwater's campaign in 1964. Then in 1966, without holding prior political office, Reagan was elected governor of California. Though he failed to win the Republican nomination for the presidency in 1976, Reagan was not discouraged and won not only the nomination, but also the White House in 1980.

Let's look at Benjamin Franklin's life. Benjamin Franklin's life is the pattern from which all other self-made men have been cut. His rhetoric of hard work, ambition, and thrift was not merely a philosophy he preached; it was the code by which he lived his life. None of his successes came by chance; they were created by the ceaseless way in which he organized his life to maximize productivity. Such discipline was necessary if he ever hoped to rise from his humble beginnings.

"If you can't tolerate stress, you can't handle success." – Niranjan Jha Showman

Franklin was the 15th of 17 children born to father Josiah Franklin, a candle-maker. Granted only two years of formal schooling, Franklin supplemented his knowledge by constantly having his nose stuck in a book. When he was 17, young Ben travelled to Philadelphia. Unlike other aristocrats of the period, who used slave labour to free up time for their other pursuits, Franklin created an enormously successful printing business which allowed him to retire and became a veritable Renaissance man.

His accomplishments are too numerous to list. As an author he penned the Poor Richard's Almanack, his famous autobiography, and numerous classic essays which got famous in the world. As an inventor, he created the lightning rod, the glass harmonica, the Franklin stove, bifocal glasses, and the flexible urinary catheter. As a thinker he established the Junto discussion group, the first subscription library, and the American Philosophical Society. As a scientist he made important investigations into the nature of electricity. He served his country, state, and city as a councilman, postmaster, and recruiter of the Pennsylvania militia, Speaker of the Pennsylvania State House, delegate to the Second Continental Congress, ambassador to France, President of Pennsylvania, and Founding Father. Not bad for the son of a candle-maker.

Chapter 3

Can You Believe It?

Johny depp: He is a famous American actor and musician. He is the recipient of multiple accolades, including a Golden Globe Award as well as nominations for three Academy Awards and two BAFTA awards. His films, in which he has often played eccentric characters, have grossed over $8 billion worldwide, making him one of Hollywood's most bankable stars. But his journey didn't begin smoothly. As a youngster, he worked as a phone salesman for branded pens. Depp donned makeup for his gig in a KISS tribute band and also dressed up as part of the faux B-52s, as well as Iggy Pop. Back then, Depp pocketed about $25 on bad nights; now he makes about $25 million per year. Jim Carrey: Before he had people in stitches, this funny guy worked as a janitor mopping floors at a tire factory. He took the job at age 15 after his father became unemployed. Carrey also had another job as a security guard. The comedian credits his early lessons in strife and toil for instilling his love of comedy.

He visited local comedy clubs to relieve stress. Michael Douglas: He is known around the world, but his beginning wasn't smooth. The New Jersey-born actor really did live the blue-collar life for a hot minute when he got his first job as a gas-station attendant. When you are in a situation of have-to-do, only then you know much you can do. A journey of a thousand miles begins with a single step. There are many people in the world who have made a major mark on society through their actions or through succeeding against all odds.

"When all else is lost, the future still remains." – Bovee

Rowan Atkinson

Rowan Atkinson is known as the world famous comedian Mr. Bean.
He was born in 1955 at Durham, England, United Kingdom.
His father Eric was a farming company director.
He graduated from Queen's College, Oxford in Electrical Engineering.
Rowan initially acted for Oxford University dramatic society.
He was first starred in a BBC comedy show named 'Atkinson People'.
Atkinson also worked for James Bond movie Never Say Never Again.
Mr. Bean, a half hour comedy show first appeared on TV in 1990.
He also worked for Just For Laughs, and then got two movies.
Rowan became a super comedian from the movie Johnny English.
His other famous movies are Rat Race, Love Actually, Ultimate Disaster.
Rowan married Sunetra Sastry who was working as a BBC makeup artist.
He was formerly in relationship with actress Leslie Ash.

Never Judge Anyone

A doctor entered the hospital in hurry after being called in for an urgent surgery. He answered the call ASAP, changed his clothes and went directly to the surgery block. He found the boy's father going and coming in the hall waiting for the doctor. Once seeing him, the dad yelled: "Why did you take all this time to come? Don't you know that my son's life is in danger? Don't you have the sense of responsibility?" The doctor smiled and said: "I am sorry, I wasn't in the hospital. I came as fastest as I could after receiving the call…… And now, I wish you'd calm down so that I can do my work."

"Calm down? What if your son was in this room right now, would you calm down? If your own son dies now what will you do?" said the father angrily. The doctor smiled again and replied: "I will say what Job said in the Holy Bible "From dust we came, and to dust we return, blessed be the name of God". Doctors cannot prolong lives. Go and intercede for your son, we will do our best by God's grace."

"Giving advice when we're not concerned is so easy." murmured the father. The surgery took some hours after which the doctor went out happy, "Thank God! Your son is saved!" And without waiting for the father's reply he carried on his way running. "If you have any question, ask the nurse!" "Why is he so arrogant? He couldn't wait some minutes so that I ask about my son's state." commented the father when seeing the nurse minutes after the doctor left. The nurse answered, tears coming down her face: "His son died yesterday in a road accident, he was in the burial when we called him for your son's surgery. And now that he saved your son's life, he left running to finish his son's burial." So, never judge a person from the present situation.

"So often we live our lives in chains and we never even know we have the key." – Seneka

Improve Your Behaviour

At intervals during the day practice thinking a carefully selected series of peaceful thoughts. Let mental pictures of the most peaceful scenes you have ever witnessed pass across your mind, as, for example, some beautiful valley filled with the hush of evening time, as the shadows lengthen and the sun sinks to rest. Or recall the silvery light of the moon falling upon rippling waters or remember the sea washing gently upon soft shores of sand. Such peaceful thought images will work upon your mind as a healing medicine. So now and then during every day allow motion pictures of peace slowly to cross your mind.

Practice the technique of suggestive articulation, that is, repeat audibly some peaceful words. Words have profound suggestive power, and there is healing in the very saying of them. Utter a series of panicky words and your mind will immediately go into a mild state of nervousness. You will perhaps feel a sinking in the pit of your stomach that will affect your entire physical mechanism. If, on the contrary, you speak peaceful, quieting words, your mind will react in a peaceful manner. Use such a word as "tranquillity." Repeat that word slowly several times. Tranquillity is one of the most beautiful and melodic of all English words, and the mere saying of it tends to induce a tranquil state.

Another healing word is "serenity." Picturize serenity as you say it. Repeat it slowly and in the mood of which the word is a symbol. Words such as these have a healing potency when used in this manner. It is also helpful to use lines from poetry or passages from the Scriptures. A man of my acquaintance who achieved a remarkable peace of mind has the habit of writing on cards unusual quotations expressing peacefulness. He carries one of the cards in his wallet at all times, referring to it frequently until each quotation is committed to memory. He says that each such idea dropped into the subconscious "lubricates" his mind with peace. A peaceful concept is indeed oil on troubled thoughts. One of the quotations which he used is from a sixteenth-century mystic, "Let nothing disturb you. Let nothing frighten you. Everything passes away except God. God alone is sufficient." The words of the Bible have a particularly strong therapeutic value. Drop them into your mind, allowing them to "dissolve" in consciousness, and they will spread a healing balm over your entire mental structure. This is one of the simplest processes to perform and also one of the most effective in attaining peace of mind.

<u>In Case of Severe Stress</u>

Some of the many causes of work-related stress include long hours, heavy workload, job insecurity and conflicts with co-workers or bosses. Symptoms include a drop in work performance, depression, anxiety and sleeping difficulties. In this case it is important to recognise work-related stress as a significant health and safety issue. A company can and should take steps to ensure that employees are not subjected to unnecessary stress.

"Two heads are better than one, but not if both are stupid." – Lincoln

Work-related stress is a growing problem around the world that affects not only the health and wellbeing of employees. This stress can be caused by various events. For example, a person might feel under pressure if the targets of their job are greater than they can comfortably manage. Other sources of work-related stress include conflict with co-workers or bosses, constant change, and threats to job security, such as potential redundancy. Antidepressant medicines help relieve the symptoms of depression and anxiety. They work by correcting chemical imbalances of neurotransmitters in the brain. Experts believe these are responsible for changes in mood and behaviour. They're mainly prescribed to treat depression, particularly persistent or severe cases, and are often used in combination with a talking therapy such as cognitive behavioural therapy (CBT). One can get this medicine only on registered doctors' prescription.

It would be too simplistic to say that depression and related mental health conditions are caused by low serotonin levels, but a rise in serotonin levels can improve symptoms and make people more responsive to other types of treatment, such as CBT. The number of people who are suffering from some kind of mental health issue is on the rise and accordingly, it has increased the number of companies who are working to provide an effective solution to the same problem. The antidepressants are made of lithium salt which has the ability to control stress related chemical reaction in human mind and tranquilize it.

Amitril-25 Tablets
Duloser-20 Tablets
Exilite Forte Tablets
Exilite-10 Tablets

Story – Dr. Jack and Mr. Hide

Dr. Jack was a very famous physician in Australia. One day, after long research, he invents a medicine that makes a good person bad, and a bad person good. Before giving it out for public use, he wants to try on himself. Dr. Jack prepares two glasses of medicine in night, drinks one and he becomes bad. Then he takes a rod in hand, goes out in dark streets, and starts beating people vehemently. All berserk, he comes home, drinks the second glass and becomes good. And nobody suspects him. But now he gets addicted to it.

Then next day, and every day, he continues beating people in night and gains the name as Mr. Hide. It becomes his habit and he enjoys tremendously. One day, being in a hurry, he prepares only one glass of medicine instead of two. He forgets to prepare the second glass, drinks the first glass, and goes out to beat people. After an hour, when he comes home and looks for the second glass, he finds nowhere. As he had become bad, he didn't know how to prepare the second glass. In exasperation, Mr. Hide cries and starts beating his head against the wall. And after a while, he dies with bleeding head.

"Two third of human existence is wasted in hesitation and last third in repentance." – Souvestre

Practical Ways of Life

There are other practical ways by which you can develop serenity and quiet attitudes. One way is through your conversation. Depending upon the words we use and the tone in which we use them, we can talk ourselves into being nervous, high-strung, and upset. We can talk ourselves into either negative or positive results. By our speech we can also achieve quiet reactions. Talk peaceful to be peaceful. In a group when the conversation takes a trend that is upsetting, try injecting peaceful ideas into the talk. Note how it counteracts the nervous tensions. Conversation filled with expressions of unhappy expectation, at breakfast, for example, often sets the tone of the day. Little wonder things turn out according to the unhappy specifications. Negative conversation adversely affects circumstances. Certainly, talk of a tense and nervous nature enhances inner agitation. On the contrary, start each day by affirming peaceful, contented, and happy attitudes and your days will tend to be pleasant and successful. Such attitudes are active and definite factors in creating satisfactory conditions. Watch your manner of speech if you wish to develop a peaceful state of mind. It is important to eliminate from conversations all negative ideas, for they tend to produce tension and annoyance inwardly.

For example, when you are with a group of people at a luncheon, do not comment that the "Communists will soon take over the country." In the first place, Communists are not going to take over the country, and by so asserting you create a depressing reaction in the minds of others. It undoubtedly affects digestion adversely. The depressing remark colours the attitude of all present, and everyone goes away with a perhaps slight but definite feeling of annoyance. They also carry away with them a mild but definite feeling that something is wrong with everything. There are times when we must face these harsh questions and deal with them objectively and vigorously, and no one has more contempt for Communism than I have, but as a general thing to have peace of mind, fill your personal and group conversations with positive, happy, optimistic, satisfying expressions.

The words we speak have a direct and definite effect upon our thoughts. Thoughts create words, for words are the vehicles of ideas. But words also affect thoughts and help to condition if not to create attitudes. In fact, what often passes for thinking starts with talk. Therefore, if the average conversation is scrutinized and disciplined to be sure that it contains peaceful expressions, the result will be peaceful ideas and ultimately, therefore, a peaceful mind. Another effective technique in developing a peaceful mind is the daily practice of silence. Everyone should insist upon not less than a quarter of an hour of absolute quiet every twenty-four hours. Go alone into the quietest place available to you and sit or lie down for fifteen minutes and practice the art of silence. Do not talk to anyone. Do not write. Do not read. Think as little as possible. Throw your mind into neutral. Conceive of your mind as quiescent, inactive. This will not be easy at first because thoughts are stirring up your mind, but practice will increase your efficiency. Conceive of your mind as the surface of a body of water and see how nearly quiet you can make it, so that there is not a ripple. When you have attained a quiescent state, then begin to listen for the deeper sounds of harmony and beauty and of God that are to be found in the essence of silence.

"Try to get what you want, otherwise you'll be forced to like what you get." - Swett Marden

Perhaps our lack of inner peace is due to some extent to the effect of noise upon the nervous system of modern people. Scientific experiments show that noise in the place where we work, live, or sleep reduces efficiency to a noticeable degree. Contrary to popular belief, it is doubtful if we ever completely adjust our physical, mental, or nervous mechanisms to noise. No matter how familiar a repeated sound becomes, it never passes unheard by the subconscious.

Marvan Atapattu

Marvan Atapattu is the rarest and prolific batsman of Sri Lanka.
He has scored five thousand runs in Test matches.
His career is considered crucial in the world of cricket.
Marvan was born in 1970 in Kalutara, Sri Lanka.
At the age of twenty, he entered international cricket.
But in his initial six years, he could score only 1 run.
He was insulted and dismissed two times form his team.
Marvan was considered not-made for international cricket.
But his good score in domestic matches got him a chance again.
For the next 11 innings, he could not score above 29 runs.
But in his tenth match against India, he hit first century.
He registered highest Test score of 249 runs against Zimbabwe.
Atapattu is also a skilful fielder with an accurate throw.
Marvan Atapattu has made 16 centuries and 6 double centuries.

In the circumstances of modern life, with its acceleration of pace, the practice of silence is admittedly not so simple as it was in the days of our forefathers. A vast number of noise-producing gadgets exist that they did not know, and our daily program is more hectic. Space has been annihilated in the modern world, and apparently, we are also attempting to annihilate the factor of time. It is only rarely possible for an individual to walk in deep woods or sit by the sea or meditate on a mountaintop or on the deck of a vessel in the midst of the ocean. But when we do have such experiences, we can print on the mind the picture of the silent place and the feel of the moment and return to it in memory to live it over again just as truly as when we were actually in that scene. In fact, when you return to it in memory the mind tends to remove any unpleasant factors present in the actual situation. The memory visit is often an improvement over the actual for the mind tends to reproduce only the beauty in the remembered scene. For example, as I write these words, I am on a balcony of one of the most beautiful hotels in the world, the Royal Hawaiian on the famed and romantic Waikiki Beach in Honolulu, Hawaii. I am looking into a garden filled with graceful palm trees, swaying in the balmy breeze.

"You will be ashamed of your death if you fail to make your life worthwhile." – Niranjan Jha Showman

The air is laden with the aroma of exotic flowers. Hibiscus, of which on these islands there are two thousand varieties, fill the garden. Outside my windows are papaya trees laden with ripening fruit. The brilliant colour of the royal poinciana, the flame of the forest trees, adds to the glamor of the scene; and the acacia trees are hung heavily with their exquisite white flowers. So you believe in what you are doing, and you too will see the great effect of your belief upon those whom you may request to help you.

Nine Motives of Human Life

Let us look at some of the other "control levers" which combine with a positive mental attitude to give you wealth and peace of mind for an entire, victorious lifetime. The nine major motives. It is not for nothing that court trials often concern themselves with questions of motive. Everything you do is the result of one or more motives. In various combinations we use nine basic motives. The seven positive motives are:

1. The emotion of LOVE
2. The emotion of SEX
3. The desire for MATERIAL GAIN
4. The desire for SELF-PRESERVATION
5. The desire for FREEDOM OF BODY AND MIND
6. The desire for SELF-EXPRESSION
7. The desire for PERPETUATION OF LIFE AFTER DEATH

The two negative emotions are:
I. The emotion of ANGER AND REVENGE
2. The emotion of FEAR

In those nine motives you can find the roots of everything you do or refrain from doing. Peace of mind is attained only by the exercise of the seven positive motives as a general pat- tern of life. Rarely if ever does a person who has peace of mind exercise the two negative motives or emotions. You cannot have peace of mind while you fear anything or anyone. You cannot have peace of mind while you entertain the kind of anger which brings you to a desire for revenge or a desire to injure another, no matter what the justification may seem to be. Great men have no time to waste with a desire to injure others. If they did, they would not be great men. Great men are not immune to fear, but theirs is not the kind of fear that hangs on constantly and takes over all of life. Look to small, mean men to see lifelong patterns of fear and anger. Their minds are so filled with these negative influences that they cannot find the power to shape the circumstances they desire.

"Don't pity me if I don't have eyes but pity them who have no vision.' – Milton

Empowering Yourself

Life is a challenge - meet it. Life is a gift - accept it. Life is an adventure - dare it. Life is a sorrow - overcome it. Life is a tragedy - face it. Life is a duty - perform it. Life is a game - play it. Life is a mystery - unfold it. Life is a song - sing it. Life is an opportunity - take it. Life is a journey - complete it. Life is a promise - fulfil it. Life is a beauty - praise it. Life is a struggle - fight it. Life is a goal - achieve it. Life is a puzzle - solve it. Life is eternal - believe it.

I've learned that no matter what happens, or how bad it seems today, life does go on, and it may be better tomorrow. I've learned that you can tell a lot about a person by the way he or she handles a rainy day and lost luggage. I've learned that regardless of your relationship with your parents, you'll miss them when they're gone from your life. I've learned that life sometimes gives you a second chance. I've learned that you shouldn't go through life with a catcher's mitt on both hands. You need to be able to throw something back. I've learned that whenever I decide something with an open heart, I usually make the right decision. I've learned that even when I have pains, I don't have to be one. I've learned that every day you should reach out and touch someone. People love that human touch - holding hands, a warm hug, or just a friendly pat on the back. I've learned that I still have a lot to learn.

A lady was giving a beautiful speech in a seminar. She was saying that there is a huge difference between growing older and growing up. If you are nineteen years old and lie in bed for one full year and don't do one productive thing, you will turn twenty years old. If I am eighty-seven years old and stay in bed for a year and never do anything I will turn eighty-eight. Anybody can grow older. That doesn't take any talent or ability. The idea is to grow up by always finding the opportunity in change.

The elderly usually don't have regrets for what we did, but rather for things we did not do. The only people who fear death are those with regrets. She concluded her speech by courageously singing The Rose. She challenged each of us to study the lyrics and live them out in our daily lives. At the year's end Rose finished the college degree she had begun all those years ago. One week after graduation Rose died peacefully in her sleep. Over two thousand college students attended her funeral in tribute to the wonderful woman who taught by example that it's never too late to be all you can possibly be.

Recently I heard about a man, now seventy, who fifteen years ago lost all his money in a real estate venture. Taking the advice of a friend, he had borrowed heavily in order to invest in vacant swampland on the assumption that in a couple of years the land would be in great demand for building lots. This did not transpire, the man's notes became due, and he had to see his retail shoe business sold out from under him. The friend who had badly advised him also had lost money. Nevertheless this man became filled with hatred toward his friend and said he would get even "if it's the last thing I do." It nearly was.

"A smooth sea never made a skilful mariner." - English proverb

Five years of hatred left him incapable even of doing business. Meanwhile the friend prospered and seemed far out of reach of any puny revenge. The man who had lost his money at length lost the balance wheel of his mind and had to spend six months in a quiet place in the country surrounded by a high wall. In his last month of confinement, however, he was sufficiently recovered to listen to an adviser who pointed out to him that hatred and the desire for revenge had done him far more harm than had been done by his losing his money.

He was persuaded to forgive the friend who had led him into the real estate deal. He even wrote to this man, telling of his change of heart. When he went back into business it was with love of his fellow men and the determination to keep his mind filled with positive, constructive motives. Beginning at the age of sixty, he built a new career. Now, at seventy, he is fairly well off, and most of all he has peace of mind, the one form of wealth which is indispensable.

Story – Alcoholic

Punjab had fallen badly in liquor addiction. A lot of social activities were going on to make people aware of the bad effect of liquor. One day, a doctor is called in a college to demonstrate about the harmfulness of alcohol. Among a big audience, he goes to the stage and puts two glasses on a table. He fills one with distilled water, and the second with liquor. Then he puts an earthworm in the first glass and let the audience see. Now the doctor puts the same earthworm in the second glass. The worm dies instantly.

He lets the viewers see the glass with dead worm. Now he probes: So have you all understood how liquor can affect our body? One among the audience responds: Yes, if we drink liquor, it will kill all worms of stomach. The doctor gets angry on the wrong perception of the viewers. In the second demonstration, he brings a donkey on the stage and lets it drink liquor. As the donkey does not drink, so he asks firmly: Now do you all see? Another one replies: Yes, who doesn't drink liquor is a donkey.

<u>Power of thinking</u>

Average people think money is the root of all evil. Rich people believe poverty is the root of all evil. Average people have a lottery mentality. Rich people have an action mentality. Average people think the road to riches is paved with formal education. Rich people believe in acquiring specific knowledge. Many world-class performers have little formal education, and have amassed their wealth through the acquisition and subsequent sale of specific knowledge. The masses are convinced that master's degrees and doctorates are the way to wealth, mostly because they are trapped in the linear line of thought that holds them back from higher levels of consciousness. The wealthy aren't interested in the means, only the end. Average people long for the good old days. Rich people dream of the future.

"It is hard to set those fools free who respect their chains." – Voltaire

Self-made millionaires get rich because they're willing to bet on themselves and project their dreams, goals and ideas into an unknown future. You need to understand the fact that the average person has been brainwashed to believe rich people are lucky or dishonest. That's why there's a certain shame that comes along with "getting rich" in lower-income communities. The world class knows that while having money doesn't guarantee happiness, it does make your life easier and more enjoyable. The rich go out and try to make them happy. They don't try to pretend to save the world. If you're not taking care of you, you're not in a position to help anyone else. You can't give what you don't have.

People who believe their best days are behind them rarely got rich, and often struggle with unhappiness and depression. Average people long for the good old days. Rich people dream of the future. Average people see money through the eyes of emotion. Rich people think about money logically. An ordinarily smart, well-educated and otherwise successful person can be instantly transformed into a fear-based, scarcity driven thinker whose greatest financial aspiration is to retire comfortably. The middle class people wait for God, government, their boss or their spouse for financial gain. Average people earn money doing things they don't love. Rich people follow their passion.

Chinese Silk Secret

The Chinese, who discovered silk making, had kept it a secret for centuries. The other countries were completely ignorant of it even though silk products had become famous in the entire world. The craving to know about silk making was mostly among Japanese as being the neighbour also they hadn't been able to crack the secret. They were waiting for the time to get them know about it. Years after years were passing. In one summer, an infectious disease spread in a village of a borderland of China. The disease was chickenpox. The entire village sank in fear as they had no cure of it. They started trying all the ways to find out the medication. From a reliable source they came to know that Japanese had a cure of that disease. Just the day after next, the two physicians from Japan were called in. The doctors checked the patients and asked how they had got the infection. In reply they said that they work in a silk mill so they might have been infected from there, because they spent most of the times of the days working there only.

Feeling at the point of catching larks, the duo asked how they made silk products. This time the Chinese denied answering saying that secret they never reveal to an outlander. The Japs, climbing up the ladder of cleverness, said that unless they know how silk is made, they won't be able to figure out the infectivity. Thinking that saving life is more important than keeping a thing secret, they revealed everything to the Japs. After the duo head everything, in a turn to tell the cure, they said to take a complete bed-rest for two weeks. The moment the villagers head this, they got angry. They said: You could have told this to us even before asking us to reveal the centuries-old secret. On that, the Japs replied: To know your secret, we had knitted this secret that we know the cure of chickenpox.

Every human life on earth is warfare. - Martin Luther King

Chapter 4

<u>Way of Thinking is Way of Living</u>

Remember that middle class take jobs they don't enjoy because they need the money and they've been trained in school and conditioned by society to live in a linear thinking world that equates earning money with physical or mental effort. Average people set low expectations so they're never disappointed. Psychologists and other mental health experts often advise people to set low expectations for their life to ensure they are not disappointed. But rich people are up for the challenge. No one would ever strike it rich and live their dreams without huge expectations. Average people believe you have to DO something to get rich. Rich people believe you have to BE something to get rich. That's why people like Donald Trump go from millionaire to nine billion dollars in debt and come back richer than ever.

While the masses are fixated on the doing and the immediate results of their actions, the great ones are learning and growing from every experience, whether it's a success or a failure. Knowing their true reward is becoming a success machine that eventually produces outstanding results. Average people live beyond their means. Rich people live below theirs. The rich live below their means, not because they're so savvy, but because they make so much money that they can afford to live like royalty while still having a king's ransom socked away for the future. Average people teach their children how to survive. Rich people teach their kids to get rich. Rich parents teach their kids from an early age about world of "haves" and "have-nots". The People say parents are teaching their kids to look down on the masses because they're poor. This isn't true. What they're teaching their kids is to see the world through the eyes of objective reality—the way society really is. If children understand wealth early on, they'll be more likely to strive for it later in life.

Story – The Telephone Lineman

This is the story of a boasting manager. There was a manager in an office and he had the nature of dominating over his staffs. One day he brings a calendar in his office and hangs on the wall. The calendar reads: I'm your boss, you have to follow me. In evening, his wife comes to the office when he was in meeting. She enters the meeting room and asks: Give me my calendar back. Feeling ashamed, the manager gives the calendar to his wife. When the owner of the company comes to know about his nature, he transfers him to a different branch.

Sitting in his new cabin of the first day in morning, the manager hears a knock at the door. He wants to impress the visitor, and so he picks up the receiver of his phone. He starts boasting about big financial transactions on the phone. By the time, the visitor gets in and stands near his table in waiting. Now he puts down the receiver and asks the visitor what brings him here? The receiver says: I'm a telephone lineman, and I am here to connect your phone to the line.

"The soul of human being is greater than his luck." – Arindam Chaudhuri

Reliance

Dhirubhai Ambani is the founder of Reliance.
He founded this company in 1954 in Ahmadabad, Gujarat, India.
He was born in 1932 in a low income family of Chorwad, Gujarat.
His father Hirachand was a school teacher at Chorwad.
Dhirubhai's first work was to sell potato fries on weekends.
He went to Aden (Greece) to work after matriculation.
He learnt English grammar and essay writing.
Dhirubhai opened the first textile mill Ahmadabad in 1954.
He started selling polyester cloth from Masjid Bunder, Mumbai.
Reliance established its first plant in 1982 competing Bombay Dying.
He also had enmity with Indian Express newspaper.
Dhirubhai Ambani is considered the great wealth creator.

Ten Habits of Successful People

Most people have habits—some are positive, some are not. Successful people tend to have more of the kinds of habits that contribute to their success. The good news, for those who wish to be successful, is that cultivating positive habits takes no more effort than developing bad ones. Some of the best habits of successful people involve only conscious effort, like getting up early every day. Others, such as becoming organized, may take a little more skill and practice but ultimately result in the most desired outcome of all—success.

Aside from the random element of fortune, much of what makes some people successful involves the cultivating of certain habits. Learning what these habits are and how to employ them in your own life is worthwhile. Here are ten habits of successful people:

1. Organizing
2. Relaxing
3. Taking Action
4. Personal Care
5. Positive Attitude
6. Networking
7. Frugality
8. Rising Early
9. Sharing
10. Reading

"Your desire for success should be greater than your fear for failure." – Bill Cosby

A Real Successful Man

A real successful man is he who attains far greater success than his original circumstances would have indicated was possible. The self-made man often has to overcome great obstacles to achieve his goals. They attain their success through education, hard work, and sheer willpower. While no man is an island, it's not external help or special relationships that make the crucial difference in the self-made man's rise. Society loves the story of a man whose success came to him largely by chance, from an opportunity dropped from the sky. Such stories allow unsuccessful men to excuse their failure as due to unavoidable bad luck and demerit the success of others by chalking their achievements up to chance.

Sadly, too many men today believe that lounging on the shore, waiting for their ship to come in, constitutes the best pathway to reaching their goals. Instead, self-made men throughout history have made their own way in life by reaching deep inside and through willpower and elbow grease, creating their own destiny. While there are always many factors to success, all are subordinate to work, which is the great key to success. So, if you love your life, then do not squander time; for that's the stuff life is made of.

<u>Facts to Learn</u>

- Master blaster cricketer Sachin Tendulkar never attended a college.
- Reliance founder Dhirubhai Ambani was only 16 when he left for Aden to work as a clerk owing to financial issues in family.
- WikiLeaks founder Julian Assange attended the University of Melbourne, majoring in physics and mathematics. He received only a minimum grade for math and left the university soon to start his own venture.
- American aviator Charles Lindbergh, the first person to fly solo across the Atlantic Ocean, quit the University of Wisconsin and took flying classes instead.
- Genius director Quentin Tarantino is a high school dropout who went to work in a video store for his love for movies.
- Steven Spielberg was not known for his academic excellence. Interestingly, he even failed to get admission into a film-making institute!
- Sir Richard Branson had a difficult time in school because of his dyslexia. He left school when he was only 16.
- Doris Lessing, won the Nobel Prize for Literature in 2007, had to end her formal schooling when she was 14. She had worked as a nanny, telephone operator, stenographer, and a journalist before becoming a novelist at the age of 31.
- Fashion designer Ralph Lauren, the founder of Polo, left the City College of New York business school to design ties for Beau Brummel. He launched Polo later that same year.

"I don't measure a man's success by how high he climbs but how high he bounces when he hits bottom." – George S. Patton

True Story of Athlete Glenn Cunningham

The little country schoolhouse was heated by an old-fashioned, pot-bellied coal stove. This little boy Glenn had the job of coming to school early each day to start the fire and warm the room before his teacher and his classmates arrived. One morning they arrived to find the schoolhouse engulfed in flames. They dragged the unconscious little boy out of the flaming building more dead than alive. He had major burns over the lower half of his body and was taken to a nearby county hospital.

From his bed the dreadfully burned, semi-conscious little boy faintly heard the doctor talking to his mother. The doctor told his mother that her son would surely die as the terrible fire had devastated the lower half of his body. But the brave boy didn't want to die. He made up his mind that he would survive. Somehow, to the amazement of the physician, he did survive. When the mortal danger was past, he again heard the doctor and his mother speaking quietly. The mother was told that since the fire had destroyed so much flesh in the lower part of his body, it would almost be better if he had died, since he was doomed to be a lifetime cripple with no use at all of his lower limbs.

Once more the brave boy made up his mind. He would not be a cripple. He would walk. But unfortunately from the waist down, he had no motor ability. His thin legs just dangled there, all but lifeless. Ultimately he was released from the hospital. Every day his mother would massage his little legs, but there was no feeling, no control, nothing. Yet his determination that he would walk was as strong as ever. When he wasn't in bed, he was confined to a wheelchair. One sunny day his mother wheeled him out into the yard to get some fresh air. This day, instead of sitting there, he threw himself from the chair. He pulled himself across the grass, dragging his legs behind him.

He worked his way very hard to the white picket fence bordering their lot. With great effort, he raised himself up on the fence. Then, stake by stake, he began dragging himself along the fence, resolved that he would walk. He started to do this every day until he wore a smooth path all around the yard beside the fence. There was nothing he wanted more than to develop life in those legs. Ultimately through his daily massages, his iron persistence and his resolute determination, he did develop his desired ability to stand up, then to walk haltingly, then to walk by himself – and then – to run.

He began to walk to school, then to run to school, to run for the sheer joy of running. Later in college he made the track team. Still later in Madison Square Garden this young man who was not expected to survive, who would surely never walk, who could never hope to run – this determined young man, Dr. Glenn Cunningham, ran the world's fastest mile! On June 16, 1934, Glenn Cunningham ran the mile in 4:06.8 minutes, breaking the world's record.

"If you are not praised or criticized, you're born for population counting." – Niranjan Jha Showman

Fill Your Mind with Experiences

Fill your mind with all peaceful experiences possible, then make planned and deliberate excursions to them in memory. You must learn that the easiest way to an easy mind is to create an easy mind. This is done by practice, by the application of the simple principles outlined here. The mind quickly responds to teaching and discipline. You can make the mind give you back anything you want but remember the mind can give back only what it was first given. Saturate your thoughts with peaceful experiences, peaceful words and ideas, and ultimately you will have a storehouse of peace- producing experiences to which you may turn for refreshment and renewal of your spirit. It will be a vast source of power.

I spent a night with a friend who has a very lovely home. We had breakfast in a unique and interesting dining room. The four walls are painted in a beautiful mural picturing the countryside in which my host was reared as a boy. It is a panorama of rolling hills, gentle valleys, and singing streams, the latter clean and sun speckled, and babbling over rocks. Winding roads meander through pleasant meadows. Little houses dot the landscape. In a central position is a white church surmounted by a tall steeple. As we breakfasted my host talked of this region of his youth, pointing out various points of interest in the painting around the wall. Then he said, "Often as I sit in this dining room I go from point to point in my memory and relive other days.

I recall, for example, walking up that lane as a boy with bare feet, and I can remember how the clean dust felt between my toes. I remember fishing in that trout stream on many a summer afternoon and coasting down those hills in the wintertime. "There is the church I attended as a boy." He grinned and said, "I sat through many a long sermon in that church but gratefully recall to mind the kindliness of the people and the sincerity of their lives. I can sit here and look at that church and think of the hymns I heard there with my mother and father as we sat together in the pew. They are long buried in that cemetery alongside the church, but in memory I go and stand by their graves and hear them speak to me as in days gone by. I get very tired and sometimes am nervous and tense. It helps to sit here and go back to the days when I had an untroubled mind, when life was new and fresh. It does something for me. It gives me peace and the peace develops into my strength."

Perhaps we all cannot have such murals on the dining-room walls, but you can put them around the wall of your mind: pictures of the most beautiful experiences of your life. Spend time among the thoughts which these pictures suggest. No matter how busy you may be or what responsibilities you carry, this simple, rather unique practice, having proved successful in many instances, may have a beneficial effect upon you. It is an easily practiced way to a peaceful mind. You can make yourself aware of certain principles of personal guidance and guardianship; and to make these principles real and memorable, you can personalize them-see them as so many Princes in armour who stand at the doors of your mind. These Princes challenge every thought-vibration which seeks to enter.

"Frighten your fear and victory is yours." – Niranjan Jha Showman

Can You Believe It?

This is a real and exemplary story of bravery in the world which is known as Uruguayan flight crash. Uruguayan Air Force Flight 571 was the chartered flight from Montevideo city of Uruguay, bound to Santiago, Chile, that crashed in the Andes mountains on October 13, 1972. The accident and subsequent survival became known as the Andes flight disaster and the Miracle of the Andes. The inexperienced co-pilot, Lieutenant-Colonel Dante Héctor Lagurara, was piloting the aircraft at the time of the accident. He mistakenly believed the aircraft had overflown Curicó, the turning point to fly north and begin descending into Pudahuel Airport in Santiago de Chile, but failed to notice that instrument readings indicated he was still 60–70 km east of Curicó. As the aircraft began its descent it struck a mountain ridge, shearing off both wings and the tail cone.

The remaining portion of the fuselage slid down a glacier at an estimated 350 km/h and descended another 725 metres (2,379 ft) before ramming into an ice and snow mound. The flight was carrying 45 passengers and crew, including 19 members of the Old Christians Club rugby union team, along with their families, supporters and friends. Three crew members and nine passengers died immediately and several more died soon after due to the frigid temperatures and the severity of their injuries. The crash site is located at an elevation of 3,570 metres (11,710 ft) in the remote Andes mountains of western Argentina, just east of the border with Chile. Authorities overflew the crash site several times during the following days searching for the aircraft, but failed to make out the white fuselage against the snow. Search efforts were called-off after eight days of searching.

During 72 days after the crash the survivors suffered from extreme hardships, including exposure, starvation and several avalanches, which led to the deaths of 13 more passengers. The remaining passengers resorted to cannibalism to survive. As the weather improved with the arrival of late spring, two survivors, Nando Parrado and Roberto Canessa, climbed the 4,650-metre (15,260 ft) mountain peak on the western rim of the glacier cirque without any mountaineering gear whatsoever and hiked for 10 days into Chile to seek help, traveling 61 km. On 23 December 1972, two months after the crash, all 16 remaining survivors were rescued.

Ways to Strengthen Hearts

When you start working towards your goal, probably harder, you feel some discomfort in your heart. Sometimes it may frighten you and that results in quitting your work. It doesn't mean you are born with a weak heart, but it just means you need to train your heart to cope with your ambition. It could be in form of restlessness, pain or anxiety. Making small modifications to your lifestyle can add up and make your heart stronger. A cardiologist offers the simple changes you can incorporate into your daily life.

"Birds born in a cage think flying is an illness." – Alejandro Jodorowsky

Here are the ways to strengthen your heart:

A. Eat Healthy
B. Get Active
C. Stay in Average Weight
D. Read Motivational Books
E. Quit Smoking
F. Control Your Blood Pressure
G. Drink Only in Moderation
H. Manage Stress

Oprah Winfrey

Oprah Gail Winfrey was born in Mississippi, United States.
She was born to an unmarried teenage housemaid mother.
But she was raised by her grandmother in a farmland.
When she was nine years old, she was raped.
When 14, she got pregnant but the relationship broke up soon after.
Winfrey's biological father was Vernon Winfrey, a coal miner turned barber.
Her son died in infancy, she started working at a local grocery store.
Later, she got a job in radio while still in high school began anchoring news at 19.
Oprah was demoted from her anchoring job because she was not fit for television.
Her emotional ad-lib delivery eventually got her transferred to the daytime-talk-show arena.
She launched her own production company and became internationally syndicated.
After her TV talk show success, she started her own studio, O magazine, and book club.
She is also ready to launch her new Oprah Winfrey Network cable channel.
Oprah is the chairwoman and CEO of Harpo Productions.
She is the CEO, and CCO of the Oprah Winfrey Network, worth $2.4 billion.
She has been ranked the richest Afro-American of the 20th century.
Oprah is the greatest black philanthropist in American history.

How to Have Constant Energy?

How we think we feel has a definite effect on how we actually feel physically. If your mind tells you that you are tired, the body mechanism, the nerves, and the muscles accept the fact. If your mind is intensely interested, you can keep on at an activity indefinitely. Religion functions through our thoughts, in fact, it is a system of thought discipline. By supplying attitudes of faith to the mind it can increase energy. It helps you to accomplish prodigious activity by suggesting that you have ample support and resources of power.

"Hurting with truth is better than comforting with lies." – Niranjan Jha Showman

Everyone is familiar with all-out energy drain -- that exhausted day when no matter how enticing that new movie, fabulous shoe sale, or friendly barbecue, we just can't psych ourselves up to go. What can be harder to recognize is a low-grade energy drain. In this case, you may not necessarily feel the classic signs of exhaustion — like achy muscles or that all-over tired feeling. What you do experience is an increasing lack of get-up-and-go for many of the activities you used to love.

You may also find it harder to concentrate on tasks, and, eventually, you can also find your patience grows short and your level of frustration rises, even when confronted with seemingly simple challenges. If this is starting to sound familiar, take heart. Energy zappers are all around us, some obvious, some hidden. The good news: There is a way around almost all of them. Here are some tips for you: Increase Your Magnesium Intake, Walk Around, Don't Skip Breakfast, Drink More Water, Eat More Whole Grains and Less Sugar, Check Your Thyroid Function.

Chapter 5

Being Intelligent

Most of us take Albert Einstein's name as synonymous with genius, but he didn't always show such promise. Einstein did not speak until he was four and did not read until he was seven, causing his teachers and parents to think he was mentally handicapped, slow and anti-social. Eventually, he was expelled from school and was refused admittance to the Zurich Polytechnic School. It might have taken him a bit longer, but most people would agree that he caught on pretty well in the end, winning the Nobel Prize and changing the face of modern physics.

Charles Darwin gave up on having a medical career and was often chastised by his father for being lazy and too dreamy. Darwin himself wrote, "I was considered by all my masters and my father, a very ordinary boy, rather below the common standard of intellect." Perhaps they judged too soon, as Darwin today is well-known for his scientific studies.

Robert Goddard: Goddard today is hailed for his research and experimentation with liquid-fuelled rockets, but during his lifetime his ideas were often rejected and mocked by his scientific peers who thought they were outrageous and impossible. Today rockets and space travel don't seem far-fetched at all, due largely in part to the work of this scientist who worked against the feelings of the time.

Isaac Newton: Newton was undoubtedly a genius when it came to math, but he had some failings early on. He never did particularly well in school and when put in charge of running the family farm, he failed miserably, so poorly in fact that an uncle took charge and sent him off to Cambridge where he finally blossomed into the scholar we know today.

"It is not that I am so smart; it is just that I stay with problems longer." — Einstein

Socrates: Despite leaving no written records behind, Socrates is regarded as one of the greatest philosophers of the Classical era. Because of his new ideas, in his own time he was called "an immoral corrupter of youth" and was sentenced to death. Socrates didn't let this stop him and kept right on, teaching up until he was forced to poison himself.

Robert Sternberg: This big name in psychology received a C in his first college introductory psychology class with his teacher telling him that, "there was already a famous Sternberg in psychology and it was obvious there would not be another." Sternberg showed him, however, graduating from Stanford with exceptional distinction in psychology, summa cum laude, and Phi Beta Kappa and eventually becoming the President of the American Psychological Association.

Miracles in Life

Miracle is true, and sometimes it happens. Here we talk about some persons' life where miracle happened. Thomas Edison was kicked out of school for being easily distracted. He received only 3 months of formal schooling. The rest of Edison's education came from his mother's homeschooling and his reading of classic books. Though he lost nearly all of his hearing at a young age, Edison did not let this disability hinder him. He early on showed a tenacious entrepreneurial streak; he sold candy and newspapers aboard trains as a youth and then won a position as telegraph operator when he saved a station agent's son from being run over by a train. As a telegrapher, he worked 12 hours a day, 6 days a week.

Edison eagerly requested the night shift so that he could read and do his experiments during the slow evening hours of his daily life. His constant tinkering paid off; Edison came up with a myriad of inventions, including the phonograph, stock ticker, fluoroscope, and most famously, the first commercially viable incandescent lamp. He filed more than 1500 patents during his lifetime and founded 14 companies including General Electric.

Abraham Lincoln lacked connections, charisma, good looks, and formal education, and yet became one of the greatest presidents in United States history. Famously born in a one-room cabin to uneducated farmer parents, Abraham Lincoln's rise to the Presidency has long been the stuff of legend. Lincoln was almost entirely self-educated; he received only 18 months of formal schooling. He offset this disadvantage by voraciously consuming any book he could get his hands on. At age 22, Lincoln packed his meagre belongings in a canoe and paddled out on his own. He taught himself the law and became a successful attorney and state legislator in Illinois. Losing his senatorial campaign in 1858 to Stephen Douglas did not deter him from his goals; he persevered against this very same opponent to win the presidency. The rest, of course, is history. Lincoln went on to guide America through her darkest and stormiest hour.

"The best revenge is just moving on and getting over it. Don't give someone the satisfaction of watching you suffer." – Seneka

Story – Alif Laila

A long time ago, Arabia was ruled by a brave king. The king had a beautiful and beloved wife, but after some years of marriage, his wife died. In the bereavement of his wife, he gets succumbed to upset life. Many of his sympathizers advise him for remarriage, but he rejects. With passing time, his mindset changes and he gets ready for marriage. He marries a girl, and being fond of listening to stories, he tells his new wife to narrate him one. As she finishes the story, he kills her. And the next day he says that he wants to marry again.

Next day he marries again, and kills his wife after she finishes the story. Now everyday he commits the same crime. This way, he had decided to kill all women of Arabia. One day, the daughter of the king's minister decides to marry him. Her father forbids but she says that the king must be stopped. Otherwise there will be no girl left in the country. She marries the king next day and starts narrating a story on his request in night. But the story doesn't end even till early morning. The kings allows her to continue the same story next night. And this way, she continues the story for months. And with passing time, the king falls in love with her.

Can You Believe It?

José Salvador Alvarenga is a Salvadoran fisherman and author who was found on January 30, 2014, aged 36 on the Marshall Islands after spending 14 months adrift in a fishing boat in the Pacific Ocean beginning on November 17, 2012. He survived mainly on a diet of raw fish, turtles, small birds, sharks and rainwater. He swam to shore at Tile Islet, a small island that is part of Ebon Atoll, on January 30. Two locals, Emi Libokmeto and Russel Laikidrik, found him naked, clutching a knife and shouting in Spanish. He was treated in a hospital in Majuro before flying to his family home in El Salvador on February 10. Alvarenga's story was heavily reported worldwide despite initial criticism from skeptics. He is the first person in recorded history to have survived in a small boat lost at sea for more than a year.

Alvarenga was born in Garita Palmera, Ahuachapán, El Salvador. He left El Salvador in 2002 for Mexico, where he worked as a fisherman for four years, employed for a time by Villermino Rodríguez. On November 17, 2012, Alvarenga set out from the fishing village of Costa Azul, near Pijijiapan, off the coast of Chiapas, Mexico. An experienced sailor and fisherman, he was intent on a 30-hour shift of deep-sea fishing, during which he hoped to catch sharks, marlins, and sailfish. His usual fishing mate was unable to join him, so he arranged instead to bring along the inexperienced 23-year-old Ezequiel Córdoba, with whom he had not previously spoken, and whose surname he did not know. Shortly after embarking, their boat, a seven-meter skiff equipped with a single outboard motor and a refrigerator-sized icebox for storing fish, was blown off by a storm that lasted five days, during which the motor and most of the portable electronics were damaged.

"You must be the change you wish to see in the world." - Mahatma Gandhi

Though they had caught nearly 500 kilograms of fresh fish, the pair were forced to dump it overboard to make the boat manoeuvrable in the bad weather. Alvarenga managed to call his boss on a two-way radio and request help before the radio's battery died. Having neither sails nor oars, no anchor, no running lights, and no other way to contact shore, the boat began to drift across the open ocean. Much of the fishing gear was also lost or damaged in the storm, leaving them with only a handful of basic supplies and little food. The search party organized by his employer failed to find of him and gave up after two days because visibility was poor. Alvarenga managed to catch fish, turtles, jellyfish, and seabirds with his bare hands, and the pair occasionally salvaged bits of food and plastic refuse floating in the water. They collected drinking water from rainfall when possible, but more frequently were forced to drink turtle blood or their own urine.

He has said that he contemplated suicide for four days after Córdoba died, but his Christian faith prevented him from doing so. He related that Córdoba made him promise not to eat his corpse after he died, so he kept it on the boat. He sometimes spoke to the corpse and after six days, fearing he was going insane, he threw it overboard. Alvarenga reported that he saw numerous transoceanic container ships but was unable to solicit help. He kept track of time by counting the phases of the moon. After counting his 15th lunar cycle, he spotted land: a tiny, desolate islet, which turned out to be a remote corner of the Marshall Islands. On January 30, 2014, he abandoned his boat and swam to shore, where he stumbled upon a beach house owned by a local couple. Alvarenga's journey had lasted 438 days.

Come Out of Your Cobweb

Lots of people live in their mental cobweb and they never come out. Neither they quit inertia nor did their inertia let them go away. When the inertia goes stronger, people like to remain where they are, and they hate to make any change in them. Probably an unknown fear haunts them and threatens from making any change. And subsequently they never change. Recently, a worldwide survey was conducted and the only question asked was: "Would you please give your honest opinion about the solution to the food shortage in the rest of the world?" The survey was, not surprisingly, a huge failure. Because:

In Africa they didn't know what "food" meant.
In Eastern Europe they didn't know what "honest" meant.
In Western Europe they didn't know what "shortage" meant.
In China they didn't know what "opinion" meant.
In the Middle East they didn't know what "solution" meant.
In South America they didn't know what "please" meant.
And, in the USA they didn't know what "the rest of the world" meant.

"Know, only then you will know, how less you know." – Albert Einstein

In reading the lives of great men, I found that the first victory they won was over themselves. Success is to be measured not so much by the position that one has reached in life as by the obstacles which he has had to overcome while trying to succeed. It is astonishing what an effort it seems to be for many people to put their brains definitely and systematically to work. The only one that can put limits on our personal will is ourselves. Develop and encourage your will to create the forces in you. Soichiro Honda has a billion-dollar business that is Honda which began with a series of failures and fortunate turns of luck. Honda was turned down by Toyota Motor Corporation for a job after interviewing for a job as an engineer, leaving him jobless for quite some time. He started making scooters of his own at home, and spurred on by his neighbours, finally started his own business. This businessman and the company he founded is today known around the world, but as the story shows, his beginning wasn't smooth. Success, in a generally accepted sense of the term, means the opportunity to experience and to realize to the maximum the forces that are within us.

Charles Babbage, the father of computer was born on 26 December 1791 at Walworth Road, London. His father was a banking partner. Charles was born with mental illness so he couldn't attend the school but was taught by tutors. He studied mathematics deeply and became the professor of Trinity College in 1810. His father, wife, and son all died in 1827. These deaths caused him to go into mental breakdown. Still he concentrated on his aim and sought a method to calculate tables without human error. His first machine of this purpose was not completed for fund problems. He made another machine Analytical Engine in 1822 to calculate automatically, which was the beginning of computer. His half brain in kept at the Hunterian Museum in Royal College of London and other half in the Science Museum of London.

What Ambitious People Must Do?

If you have ambition, you must learn to nurture it. If you have dream, you must learn to fulfil it. And if you have manoeuvre, you must plan to apply it. All too often the motive of material gain-excellent in itself-conflicts with the excellent motive of freedom of body and mind because in gaining what is material we give up freedom of mind; we load the mind with guilt and fear because we do not act honestly. If you are ambitious, here is what you must do:

- Believe in yourself
- Quit your inertia
- Improve your trait
- Take support from people
- Sharpen your smartness
- Try to become a good speaker
- Try to become a good leader

"The future belongs to those who believe in the beauty of their dreams." – Roosevelt

The Chief Minister of Tripura, India

Here we talk about the Chief Minister of Tripura in eastern India whose name is Manik Sarkar. His life is the icon of simplicity after achieving great success. While learning about him, you'll understand that success doesn't mean the accumulation of money but the achievement you have got. Though money is necessary, but for that you should not be so greedy that you have to sell out your soul. And if you do that, you will lose the peace of mind and will have a mental breakdown soon. Here we learn about a legendary honest and successful Chief Minister of Tripura, India. His name is Manik Sarkar. He is India's only chief minister of India who doesn't own a home, a car or a bank balance worth the mention. His bank account had a balance of Rs. 6,500 on September 17, 2012.

The Chief Minister Manik Sarkar donates his salary to party fund and gets a monthly wage of Rs. 5,000 in return. His wife's pension sustains both of them. At 10 a.m. sharp, he hops into the official vehicle, which is out of bounds for even his wife, Panchali Bhattacharya, a former employee of the Central Social Welfare Board. Bhattacharya, 61, who retired last year, is often seen travelling in the capital of the state in a rickshaw without security.

The ruling Left Front's strategy for the February 2013 Assembly polls revolves around this slogan of honesty, as personified by its chief minister. Before he signs off, he has a clarification to make. "My spectacles cost Rs. 1,800. My sandals are also cheap. I love to look neat, but that doesn't mean I buy expensive stuff, says the cricket-crazy Chief Minister, who was a good batsman in college. A fan of Sachin Tendulkar, Sourav Ganguly and Mohammad Azharuddin, his current favourite is India's latest cricketing heart-throb Virat Kohli.

Story – Don't Live in Euphoria

A few years ago, a woman welfare association in Mumbai organized a program for married women. Some media personnel were also invited to telecast this show live. It was an effort to check love between husbands and wives who have busy lives in cities and get less time to communicate. They call almost fifty women to participate in the competition. They ask the participants to send an "I love you" message to their husbands and show the reply. The best reply is to win an exciting prize.

Almost fifty women send the message from their cellphones to husbands. After sometime, they start getting replies. The receiving messages are being shown on a big screen so that all can see. One gets the reply: You got fever again? Go and have some pills. The second gets the reply: I have told you to not watch horror movies, but you don't listen. But the woman who wins the prize, she gets very exhilarating response. Her husband replies: "Who?"

"Darkness cannot drive out darkness: only light can do that. Hate cannot drive out hate: only love can do that." – Martin Luther King

What is Advocacy?

In a class of law, an advocate was teaching advocacy to the students. He asks the students: Suppose two people come to me, one is clean and the other is dirty. I advise them to for a shower, now tell me who will bathe? The students say: The one who is dirty. The advocate says: No, the clean person will do because he has the habit of bathing. Now tell me who will bathe? The students say: The clean person. The advocate responds: No, the dirty person will bathe because he needs it. Now tell me who will bathe? The students say: The dirty person. The advocate adds further: No, both will bathe because the clean person has habit while the dirty one needs it. Now tell me who will bathe? The students say: Both. The advocate finally replies: Wrong, no one will bathe because dirty is not used to bathing and clean doesn't need to bathe.

Set You Goal

You must set your goal for success. Let's read this story to understand this instruction better. A farmer had a dog that used to sit by the roadside waiting for vehicles to come around. As soon as one came he would run down the road, barking and trying to overtake it. One day a neighbour asked the farmer "Do you think your dog is ever going to catch a car?" The farmer replied, "That is not what bothers me. What bothers me is what he would do if he ever caught one." Many people in life behave like that dog who is pursuing meaningless goals.

You have to set a goal in your life. Nothing good ever happens automatically rather in the wait, the situations get worst to strangle your throat. Don't think that all the opportunities of the world are gobbled up by the people who were born before you. This is the world of surprises. Many surprising thing happen here and you can also do one. Do you know that most of the American theme songs were composed by Japanese? Do you know that Indian actor Rajnikant is more famous in Japan than his own country? The Statue of Liberty and other statues of America were made by Frenchman. In the beginning, gun was slower as 12 times than bow. The first car had no back gear. The hamburger was made by German.

Here are some interesting things of language that can ignite your mind. After 500 years of the birth of Jesus Christ, some tribal people living in ANGLIA district of Germany moved out of the country and occupied a new land. As they had come from Anglia, they named themselves Angle. And so we have Angle+land as England, and Angle+ish as English. In Spanish, cock means bird and roach means fish. This word came into existence because a cockroach can both fly and swim. The picture of Monalisa is a mixed appearance of Egyptian God and Goddess of love Amon and Lisa. The painting was drawn and popularized by Leonardo Da Vinci because of his ambiguous carnal instinct. Quran is made of two words, 'Qurra' which means read, and 'Aan' which means this. So etymologically Quran means 'Read This'.

"Be yourself; everyone else is already taken." – Oscar Wilde

The reason why letter 'K' comes as a silent letter in the word 'Knife' is that this word came from French word CANIF with the same meaning. When English people were making their language, they used NIF as NIFE with symbolic letter 'K' to justify its origin. Most of the words with silent letters have the same kind of history.

Let this kind of information tickle your mind. When something happens in you, let it happens. Feel the thrill happening in your mind and let it from energy. Let it form the courage in you to believe that the world is not end after you but you can also do a lot. You can also explore. You can also find out some more truth to the world.

The History of Some Company Names

- Accenture: Accent on the future. The name Accenture was proposed by a company employee in Norway as part of an internal name finding process in January 2001. The company was called Andersen Consulting before 2001.
- Acer: Born as Multitech International in 1976, the company changed its name to Acer in 1987. This is a Latin word for sharp, acute, able and facile.
- Adidas: from the name of the founder Adi Dassler.
- Amazon.com: The founder Jeff Bezos renamed the company Amazon after the world's most voluminous river, the Amazon. He saw the potential for a larger volume of sales in an online bookstore.
- AT&T: The American Telephone and Telegraph Corporation officially changed its name to AT&T in the 1990s.
- BMW: Bayerische Motoren Werke - Bavarian Motor Works.
- Chevrolet: Named after company co-founder Louis Chevrolet, a Swiss-born auto racer. The company was merged into General Motors in 1917 and survives only as a brand name.
- Cisco: Shortened for San Francisco.
- Coca-Cola: Derived from the coca leaves and kola nuts used as flavouring. Coca-Cola creator John S. Pemberton changed the 'K' of kola to 'C' to make the name look better.
- Colgate: Colgate was named after William Colgate, an English immigrant, who set up a starch, soap and candle business in New York City in 1806.
- Ferrari: From the name of its founder, Enzo Ferrari.
- Fiat: Acronym of Fabbrica Italiana Automobili Torino - Italian Automobile Factory of Turin.
- HMV: From "His Master's Voice", this appeared in 1899 as the title of a painting of Nipper, a Jack Russell terrier, listening to a gramophone.
- Hyundai: Connotes the sense of "the present age" or "modernity" in Korean.
- IBM: Named by Tom Watson, an ex-employee of National Cash Register, NCR Corporation. To one-up them in all respects, he called his company International Business Machines.
- Intel: Robert Noyce and Gordon Moore initially incorporated their company as N M Electronics. Someone suggested Moore Noyce Electronics but it sounded too close to "more noise". Later, they changed it to Integrated Telecom.
- L&T: The Company was founded in Mumbai, India in 1938 by two Danish engineers, Henning Holck-Larsen & Soren Kristian Toubro.

"You will face many defeats in life, but never let yourself be defeated." – Maya Angelou

- <u>Nokia</u>: It started as a wood-pulp mill, the company expanded into producing rubber products in the Finnish city of Nokia. The company later adopted the city's name.
- <u>Toshiba</u>: Named from the merger of consumer goods company Tokyo Denki and electrical firm Shibaura Seisaku-sho.
- <u>Toyota</u>: From the name of the founder, Sakichi Toyoda. Initially called Toyeda, it was changed after a contest for a better-sounding name. The new name was written in katakana with eight strokes, a number that is considered lucky in Japan.
- <u>Vodafone</u>: From Voice, Data, Telefone. Vodafone made the UK's first mobile call at a few minutes past midnight on 1 January 1985.
- <u>Wipro</u>: From Western India Palm Refined Oil Ltd Wipro Technologies. The company started as a modest Vanaspati and laundry soap producer and is now also an IT services giant.

McDonald's

McDonald's is an American fast food company.
It was founded in 1940 as a restaurant in California.
This company was founded by Richard and Maurice McDonald.
McDonald's had first started selling hamburger in California.
This establishment sold it first franchise in 1955.
McDonald's is the world's largest restaurant chain.
It has 38 thousand outlets in one hundred countries.
It servers seventy million customers daily in the world.
This eatery is best known for hamburger, French fries, soft drink.
McDonald's has the ninth highest global brand value.
McDonald's franchise fee is Rs. 30 lakh in India.
In India, McDonald's has the largest outlet in Guwahati, Assam.

Knowing Reading and Knowing What to Read

People know what is reading, but they don't know what to read and how to read. Knowing what to read means you have to select the thing of your choice and read it. If there is no work in your life still reading is something that you can do. It improves both your knowledge and language. And how to read means don't read like dummies. When an idea, thought or principle creates a wave in your mind, feel it. Read everything from your heart. That is the art of reading. In today's world, the people with irresponsible mind most often say that they don't have time to do a particular work. The fact is that they are not lacking time, they are lacking MIND. They are lacking concentration. They are lacking optimism. They are lacking persistence. They are lacking motivation. And they are lacking spiritually energized peace.

"Many of life's failures are people who did not realize how close they were to success when they gave up." – Edison

There is a difference between peace and spiritually energized peace. In the search of peace, many people leave their work with support their living and get rusted away falling in tension, then frustration, and then depression. The half of the world still don't know that human mind is also affected by illness and for that there is a medical cure or spiritual energy that can drive forces into their mind to come out of mental disability. There is a way, believe me! And you have to believe because I have experienced all this in my life. When you are born, your upbringing, family atmosphere and schooling starts giving shapes to your life. From pre-teenage, you start sensing your likes and dislikes, and that make you develop an interest in you which after nurtured with time and patience becomes your talent. You have to find out what talent is there in you.

Me as Victim – Me as Winner

In my childhood, I had an inclination to reading poetries. Believe me; it began with that when I was ten years old. Because of physical weakness I was not interested in sports. Reading poetries, I started reading about the poets' life. A few years later, I started getting little linguistic about improving my first language which was not English. After a year or two, putting die-hard efforts, I started learning English and then foreign languages. And now here I am. If you say to me that if you had a mind like mine, you would have become like me, I would say that you start your efforts and you will get your mind like mine.

What we give to the people, they give us the same. We don't go anywhere but keep moving round and round. It was my reading habit that encouraged me to get optimistic to my life, otherwise I was not. The poverty I was born in, the surrounding I was brought up in and the ill-will I was instilled with, they all were ready to ruin my life. At the age of fourteen I had to learn how to use country guns. I had my involvement in a lot of devastating activities starting from narcotic consumption to immoral conduct. But there came a day when a book came in my hand authored by Swett Marden. I am immensely thankful to him to motivating my life. Then I did not stop and continued reading all motivational books. Dale Carnegie, Napoleon Hill, Arindam Chaudhary, Shiv Khera, and Lord Osho! I adore these great personalities.

I set my goal in teaching English and foreign languages, and since fifteen years I have been doing the same. There came many problems in my life. When I was a child, my family hammered me to grow and earn. And from the age of twenty when I really started scaling the tower of growth, they became a great hurdle to me. I received the unfathomable anguish from my family in marital case. The 65% happiness of your life depends upon your matrimony. I won after losing a lot. The year 2011 was a dark age of my life. I was deeply depressed seeing failure caused by my own people. Then I read somewhere the words of Will Smith: Throughout life people will make you mad, disrespect you and treat you bad. Let God deal with the things they do, because hate in your heart will consume you too. Thank you Will Smith!

"Pain never really goes away; you just elevate and get used to it by growing stronger." – Philippos

Effect of Guilt

The effect of guilt and fear feelings on energy is widely recognized by all authorities having to do with the problems of human nature. The quantity of vital force required to give the personality relief from either guilt or fear or a combination of each is so great that often only a fraction of energy remains for the discharge of the functions of living.

Energy drainage occasioned by fear and guilt is of such an amount as to leave little power to be applied to a person's job. The result is that he tires quickly. Not being able to meet the full requirements of his responsibility, he retreats into an apathetic, dull, listless condition and is indeed even ready to give up and fall back sleepily in a state of enervation. A businessman was referred to me by a psychiatrist whom the patient had been consulting. It appeared that the patient, generally regarded as quite morally strict and upright, had become involved with a married woman. He had attempted to break off this relationship but was encountering resistance from his partner in infidelity, although he had earnestly besought her to abandon their practice and allow him to return to his former state of respectability.

She had threatened him with the possibility that she might enlighten her husband concerning these escapades if he insisted in his desire to cease the relationship. The patient recognized the fact that if the husband became apprised of the situation, it would result in disgrace for him in his community. He happened to be a prominent citizen and prized his high standing. As a result of his fear of exposure and a sense of guilt, he had been unable to sleep or rest. And since this had gone on for two or three months he was in a very serious slump in energy and did not possess the vitality to perform his job efficiently. Inasmuch as some important matters were pending, the situation was serious.

When the psychiatrist suggested that he see me, a clergyman, because of his inability to sleep, he remonstrated by saying there was no way in which a clergyman could correct the condition which caused his sleeplessness, but, on the contrary, he felt that a medical doctor might supply effective medication. When he stated his attitude to me, I simply asked him how he expected to sleep when he had two very annoying and unpleasant bedfellows with whom he was attempting to sleep.

We dealt with the fear which was of exposure by the simple expedient of getting him ready in mind to face whatever might ensue as a result of doing the right thing, which was of course to break off the relationship regardless of consequences. I assured him that whatever he did that was right would turn out right. One never does wrong by doing right. I urged him to put the matter in God's hands and simply do the right thing, leaving the outcome to God. He did that, not without trepidation, but with considerable sincerity just the same. The woman, either through shrewdness or some expression of her own better nature or through the more doubtful expedient of transferring her affections elsewhere, released him.

"If life were predictable it would cease to be life and be without flavour." – Roosevelt

The guilt was handled by seeking God's forgiveness. When this is sincerely sought it is never denied, and our patient found surcease and relief. It was astonishing how when this double weight was lifted from his mind his personality once again began to function normally. He was able to sleep. He found peace and renewal of strength. Energy quickly returned. A wiser and thankful man, he became able to carry on his normal activities. A not infrequent case of diminishing energy is staleness. The pressure, monotony, and unceasing continuity of responsibilities dull the freshness of mind which a person must have to approach his work successfully. As an athlete goes stale so does the individual, whatever his occupation, who tends to come upon dry and arid periods. During such a condition of mind the expenditure of greater energy is required to do with difficulty what one formerly did with comparative ease. As a result, the vital powers are hard put to it to supply the force required, and the individual often loses his grip and power.

A solution for this state of mind was employed by a prominent business leader, president of the board of trustees of a certain university. A professor who had formerly been outstanding and extraordinarily popular had begun to slip in teaching ability and in the power to interest students. It was the verdict of the students, as well as the private opinion of the trustees, that this teacher must either recover his former capacity to teach with interest and enthusiasm or it would be necessary to replace him.

This latter expedient was entertained with hesitancy for the reason that there still remained a normal expectancy of several active years before he reached the age of retirement. The businessman above referred to ask the professor to come to his office and announced to him that the board of trustees was giving him a six months' leave of absence with all expenses paid and with full salary. There was only one stipulation, and that was that he go away to a place of rest and give himself over to gaining a complete renewal of strength and energy. The businessman invited him to use a cabin which he himself owned in a wilderness setting and made the curious suggestion that he take no books except one book, the Bible.

He suggested that the professor's daily program be walking, fishing, and some manual work in the garden; that he read the Bible every day for such a period as would enable him to read the Book through three times in the six months. He further suggested that he memorize as many passages as possible for the purpose of saturating his mind with the great words and ideas which the Book contains. The businessman said, "I believe that if you spend six months outdoors chopping wood, digging in the soil, reading the Bible, and fishing in the deep lakes you will become a new man." The professor agreed to this unique proposal. His adjustment to this radically different mode of life was an easier one than he or anyone who knew him expected. In fact, he was surprised to find that he actually liked it.

Thoughts are things, a poet said, and truly they have an existence of their own, so that a curse comes back to curse you and a blessing comes back to bless you, reflected by the mighty mirror of life. The purpose of our lives is to be happy.

"The only impossible journey is the one you never begins." – Tony Robbins

Microsoft Windows

Windows is a graphical operating system.
It is developed and marketed globally by Microsoft.
Microsoft was founded by Bill Gates and Paul Allen.
Windows was first released in 1985 as Windows 1.
This operating system is available in 110 different languages.
Before Windows, people used to work computer using MS-DOS.
This operating system spread over 90% of computer market.
It had competition with Mac operating system of Apple.
Windows' initial name was Interface Manager.
Windows XP was the best version of Windows operating system.
Microsoft has released the latest version as Windows 365.
Satya Nadella is the current CEO of Microsoft.

Refrain from Bad Things

To achieve success, you must change of habits. Many times your habit obstructs your success. You plan a lot, but your plan won't work if your habit doesn't support them. Don't spend major time with minor people. If there are people in your life who continually disappoint you, break promises, stomp on your dreams, are too judgmental, have different values and don't have your back during difficult times...that is not friendship. To have a friend, be a friend. Sometimes in life as you grow, your friends will either grow or go. Surround yourself with people who reflect values, goals interests and lifestyles. When I think of any of my successes, I am thankful to God from whom all blessings flow, and to my family and friends who enrich my life. Over the years my phone book has changed because I changed, for the better. At first, you think you're going to be alone, but after a while, new people show up in your life that makes it so much sweeter and easier to endure. Remember what your elders used to say, Birds of a feather flock together. If you're an eagle, don't hang around chickens.

Did you know that an eagle knows when a storm is approaching long before it breaks? The eagle will fly to some high spot and wait for the winds to come. When the storm hits, it sets its wings so that the wind will pick it up and lift it above the storm. While the storm rages below, the eagle is soaring above it. The eagle does not escape the storm. It simply uses the storm to lift it higher. It rises on the winds that bring the storm. When the storms of life come upon us - and all of us will experience them - we can rise above them by setting our minds and our belief toward God. The storms do not have to overcome us. We can allow God's power to lift us above them. God enables us to ride the winds of the storm that bring sickness, tragedy, failure and disappointment in our lives. We can soar above the storm. Remember, it is not the burdens of life that weigh us down; it is how we handle them.

"You only live once, but if you do it right, once is enough." – Mae West

Whatever you dwell upon in your mind, you give power to. You give your energy to it. So of course it makes sense to focus on what you want rather than what you don't want. Yet there are many ways in which the things you don't want can sneak into your thinking. Worry and doubt focus your thinking on what you don't want. Rather than worrying about the bad things that might happen, direct your actions toward making positive things happen.

Complaining can also get your mind side-tracked into thinking about what you don't want. What do you complain about? The things you don't like. Rather than complaining, take action. Action moves you toward what you do want. Anger is one more way to get your thinking negatively directed. Rather than getting angry about what you don't like, use that energy to give you determination for what you want to achieve. Keep your mind positively focused on the good things that life can offer. Those things will grow stronger and more abundant in your world.

Andrew Carnegie represents the epitome of the self-made man. His father was a Scottish hand-loom weaver, who moved with his family to America when Andrew was 13. Carnegie's first job was working as a bobbin boy at a textile factory, making $1.50 a week. He subsequently took jobs as a boiler tender, bookkeeper's clerk, and telegraph delivery boy. All the while he read to educate himself and worked to mitigate his thick Scottish accent. In 1853, Carnegie landed a job with the Pennsylvania Telegraph Co. He religiously saved his money and reinvested it in the railroad business.

He worked his way up to being superintendent of the Pennsylvania Railroad's Western Division and then supervised the Union's telegraph lines during the Civil War. He continued to make incredibly wise investments with his savings which reaped him handsome dividends. After the war, he left the railroad business and began to focus on building and investing in ironworks. By bringing great efficiency to the business, taking over one steel company after another, and utilizing vertical integration, Carnegie soon created an empire of steel and iron. In 1901, Carnegie sold his steel holdings to JP Morgan for $480 million. Carnegie had long preached what he called "The Gospel of Wealth," a philosophy in which a man should aim to acquire as much fortune as possible and then give it away to others. On this point, Carnegie was a man of his word. During his lifetime he donated $350,695,653 to philanthropic causes; upon his death he gave away the last $30,000,000 of his wealth.

Children are more expert in happiness than adults. The adult who can carry the spirit of a child into middle and old age is a genius, for he will preserve the truly happy spirit with which God endowed the young. The subtlety of Jesus Christ is remarkable, for He tells us that the way to live in this world is to have a childlike heart and mind. In other words, never get old or dull or jaded in spirit. Don't become super- sophisticated. Many of us manufacture our own unhappiness. Of course, not all unhappiness is self-created, for social conditions are responsible for not a few of our woes. Yet it is a fact that to a large extent by our thoughts and attitudes we distill out of the ingredients of life either happiness or unhappiness for ourselves.

"When injustice becomes law, resistance becomes duty." – Thomas Jefferson

Chapter 6

Try Prayer Power

In a business office high above the city streets, two men were having a serious conversation. One, heavily troubled by a business and personal crisis, paced the floor restlessly, then sat dejectedly, head in hand, a picture of despair. He had come to the other for advice, since he was considered a man of great understanding. Together they had explored the problem from every angle but seemingly without result, which only served to deepen the troubled man's discouragement. "I guess no power on earth can save me," he sighed. The other reflected for a moment, then spoke rather diffidently. "I wouldn't look at it that way. I believe you are wrong in saying there is no power that can save you. Personally, I have found that there is an answer to every problem. There is a power that can help you." Then slowly he asked, "Why not try prayer power?"

Somewhat surprised, the discouraged man said, "Of course I believe in prayer, but perhaps I do not know how to pray. You speak of it as something practical that fits a business problem. I never thought of it that way, but I'm willing to try prayer if you will show me how." He did apply practical prayer techniques and in due course got his answer. Matters ultimately turned out satisfactorily. That is not to say he did not have difficulties. In fact, he had rather a hard time of it but ultimately, he worked his way out of this trouble. Now he believes in prayer power so enthusiastically that I recently heard him say, "Every problem can be solved and solved right if you pray."

Experts in physical health and well-being often utilize prayer in their therapy. Disability, tension, and kindred troubles may result from a lack of inner harmony. It is remarkable how prayer restores the harmonious functioning of body and soul. A friend of mine, a physiotherapist, told a nervous man to whom he was giving a massage, "God works through my fingers as I seek to relax your physical body, which is the temple of your soul. While I work on your outward being, I want you to pray for God's relaxation inwardly." It was a new idea to the patient, but he happened to be in a receptive mood and he tried passing some peace thoughts through his mind. He was amazed at the relaxing effect this had on him.

Jack Smith, operator of a health club, which is patronized by many outstanding people, believes in the therapy of prayer and uses it. He was at one time a prize fighter, then a truck driver, later a taxi driver, and finally opened his health club. He says that while he probes his patrons for physical flabbiness he also probes for spiritual flabbiness because, he declares, "You can't get a man physically healthy until you get him spiritually healthy." One day Walter Huston, the actor, sat by Jack Smith's desk. He noted a big sign on the wall on which were penciled the following letters: A P R P B W P R A A. In surprise Huston asked, "What do those letters mean?"

Smith laughed and said, "They stand for 'Affirmative Prayers Release Powers By Which Positive Results Are Accomplished.'" Huston's jaw dropped in astonishment. "Well, I never expected to hear anything like that in a health club."

"Between 'Run' and 'Ruin" there is a difference of I." – Arindam Chaudhuri

Common Fobias That Victimize People

There are some common fobias that affect people during their hardwork for achieving goals. A phobia is an anxiety disorder involving excessive and persistent fear of a situation or object. Phobias typically result in a rapid onset of fear and are usually present for a long period of time. Those affected go to great lengths to avoid the situation or object, to a degree greater than the actual danger posed. If the object or situation cannot be avoided, they experience significant distress. Other symptoms can include fainting, which may occur in blood or injury phobia, and panic attacks. Typical symptoms of phobias can include nausea, trembling, rapid heartbeat, feelings of unreality, and being preoccupied with the fear object. Here is a list of some most common fobias that you make sure you don't have. And in case you have, try to kick off by psychological treatment.

- ➢ Social phobias: This phobia is marked by a fear of social situations in which a person fears of being judged or embarrassed.

- ➢ Atychiphobia: This phobia is related to an intense fear of failure. It may cause you to put off or avoid any activity or scenario that has the potential for an unsuccessful outcome. Someone with this condition may be scared to try new things, take risks or embrace growth for fear of failure.

- ➢ Glossophobia: This phobia is associated with the fear of public speaking, It is a very common phobia among children and adults and one that is believed to affect up to 75% of the population. Some individuals may feel a slight nervousness at the very thought of public speaking, while others experience full-on panic and fear.

- ➢ Nosophobia: In this a person has a persistent, irrational fear of having some disease. Nosophobia differs from illness anxiety disorder, which causes you to worry about all types of sicknesses.

- ➢ Triskaidekaphobia: It is a fear that you have a bad luck and your misfortune cannot be driven away. Those who suffer from this fear face danger due to superstitions. They may avoid starting any work without astrological or theological assurance.

- ➢ Agoraphobia – It is a fear of situations where escape is difficult. This can lead to people avoiding all sorts of wide open spaces and crowded places. It can get so severe that some sufferers end up not wanting to leave their homes at all.

Phobias are generally linked to an early negative childhood experience. For example, if you're trapped in a confined space when you're young, you may develop a fear of enclosed spaces when you're older. It's also thought that phobias can sometimes be "learnt" from an early age.

"Pressure can paralyze if a person is not prepared." - Shiv Khera

Story - An Antique Bowl

There lived a grocer in a town and he had a beautiful cat. The cat used to drink milk from an antique bowl. One day an antiquarian was passing through the way and he stops at the grocery shop. He was a good antique dealer over the years. The reason he stopped was the bowl from which the cat was drinking milk. He familiarizes himself with the grocer. Then he tells: Lalaji, I want to buy your beautiful cat. Tell me the price please.

After much bargain, the cat's price is fixed ten thousand rupees. He pays the money in cast. As he buys the cat and moves ahead, he turns back to the grocer smilingly. "You have sold your cat, so give me the bowl also," the antiquarian requests. The grocer responds: No, I won't. The dealer makes him understand that now he has no use of the bowl. But he finally reveals: Because of this bowl, I've sold fifty cats.

Believe in Your Heart

Believe in your heart that something wonderful is about to happen. Love your life. Believe in your own powers, and your own potential, and in your own innate goodness. Wake every morning with the awe of just being alive. Discover each day the magnificent, awesome beauty in the world. Explore and embrace life in yourself and in everyone you see each day. Reach within to find your own specialness. Amaze yourself and rouse those around you to the potential of each new day. Don't be afraid to admit that you are less than perfect; this is the essence of your humanity. Let those who love you help you.

Trust enough to be able to take. Look with hope to the horizon of today, for today is all we truly have. Live this day well. Let a little sun out as well as in. Create your own rainbows. Be open to all your possibilities; all possibilities and Miracles. In ancient times, a King had a boulder placed on a roadway. Then he hid himself and watched to see if anyone would remove the huge rock. Some of the king's wealthiest merchants and courtiers came by and simply walked around it. Many loudly blamed the king for not keeping the roads clear, but none did anything about getting the stone out of the way.

Then a peasant came along carrying a load of vegetables. Upon approaching the boulder, the peasant laid down his burden and tried to move the stone to the side of the road. After much pushing and straining, he finally succeeded. After the peasant picked up his load of vegetables, he noticed a purse lying in the road where the boulder had been. The purse contained many gold coins and a note from the king indicating that the gold was for the person who removed the boulder from the roadway. The peasant learned what many of us never understand. Every obstacle presents an opportunity to improve our condition.

"Don't wait for things to happen but make them happen." – Napoleon Hill

Don't be Too Stupid

Chill: What does your dad do, Jill?

Jill: He is a great man. Do you know about the Arabian Sea?

Chill: Yes, I know.

Jill: He dug a hole for it.

Chill: Oh! My dad is also great. Do you know about the Dead Sea?

Jill: Of Course!

Chill: He killed it!

Jill: Wow! Then what does he do now?

Chill: He shoots polar bears in Australia.

Jill: But there aren't any polar bear in Australia.

Chill: No? Well, he must have shot all of them.

If you plant honesty, you will reap trust. If you plant goodness, you will reap friends. If you plant humility, you will reap greatness. If you plant perseverance, you will reap victory. If you plant consideration, you will reap harmony. If you plant hard work, you will reap success. If you plant forgiveness, you will reap reconciliation. If you plant openness, you will reap intimacy. If you plant patience, you will reap improvements. If you plant faith, you will reap miracles. But if you plant dishonesty, you will reap distrust. If you plant selfishness, you will reap loneliness. If you plant pride, you will reap destruction. If you plant envy, you will reap trouble. If you plant laziness, you will reap stagnation. If you plant bitterness, you will reap isolation. If you plant greed, you will reap loss. If you plant gossip, you will reap enemies. If you plant worries, you will reap wrinkles. If you plant sin, you will reap guilt. So be careful what you plant now, it will determine what you will reap tomorrow, the seeds you now scatter, Will make life worse or better, your life or the ones who will come after.

The Singing Sensation – Akon

Akon is a famous Afro-American singer and music producer.

He was born in 1973 at Saint Louis, Missouri, USA.

His musician father Mor Thiam raised him in musical environment.

He learnt to play many instruments and settled in New Jersey.

His album 'Trouble' in 2004 and song 'Lonely' in 2005 got success.

The song reached the top five in US, UK, Australia, and Germany.

Next album came with 'Smack that' and Wanna love you' songs.

These two songs made Akon an international superstar.

Akon and Michael Jackson were close friends till the end.

Lady Gaga and T. Pain were given chance by Akon.

He has his charity for supporting orphans in Africa.

Akon also owns a diamond mine in South Africa.

"There are no limitations to the mind except those we acknowledge." – Dale Carnegie

Can You Believe It?

Let's look at the foundation story of Cambridge university. It is one of the most famous universities of the world. The start of Cambridge university is generally taken as 1209, when scholars from Oxford migrated to Cambridge to escape Oxford's riots of "town and gown" (townspeople versus scholars). To avert possible troubles, the authorities in Cambridge allowed only scholars under the supervision of a master to remain in the town. It was partly to provide an orderly place of residence that (in emulation of Oxford) the first college, Peterhouse, was founded in 1284 by Hugo de Balsham, bishop of Ely. Over the next three centuries another 15 colleges were founded, and in 1318 Cambridge received formal recognition as a studium generale from Pope John XXII.

Cambridge remained fairly insignificant until about 1502, when a professorship of divinity was founded—the oldest in the university. In 1511 Desiderius Erasmus went to Cambridge and did much to inculcate the new learning of the Renaissance there. In 1546 Henry VIII founded Trinity College (which was and still remains the largest of the Cambridge colleges). In 1570 Elizabeth I gave the university a revised body of statutes, and in 1571 the university was formally incorporated by act of Parliament. The new statutes, which remained in force for nearly three centuries, vested the effective government of the university in the heads of colleges.

Membership of the university was no longer envisaged without membership of a college. In 1663 the Lucasian professorship of mathematics was founded under the will of a former member of the university, and six years later the first holder resigned in favour of Isaac Newton, then a young fellow of Trinity. Newton held the chair for over 30 years and gave the study of mathematics a unique position in the university.

Story - Mirror Effect

An African, while moving in a forest, gets a piece of glass. Before this he hadn't seen any glass so he got attracted to it. He brings the piece home and looks into it. He sees a face inside, and assumes, that is his father. Now he starts talking to face almost every day. One day, his wife notices his talking activity and wants to investigate. When the man is out for some work, she picks up the mirror in hand and sees a face inside.

Her doubt increases and she believes this is the woman her husband talks to so often. Getting angry, she comes to her mother-in-law with the complaint. She speaks: Your son looks into this piece and talks to this woman quite frequently. The mother takes the piece in her hand to observe. She also finds a face inside but replies: You are right but you don't need to worry. This woman is very old and will die soon!

"Education is not what you know but what you are." – Indira Gandhi

There Is No Unsolvable Problem

There is no difficulty you cannot overcome. A wise and philosophical Negro man once said to me, when asked how he overcame his difficulties, "How do I get through a trouble? Well, first I try to go around it, and if I can't go around it, I try to get under it, and if I can't get under it, I try to go over it, and if I can't get over it, I just plow right through it." Then he added, "God and I plow right through it." Take seriously that formula of a businessman given earlier in this chapter. Stop reading for a moment and repeat it over to yourself five times, and each time you say it conclude with this affirmation, "I believe that." Here is the formula again, "I can do all things through Christ which strengthenth me" (Philippians 4:13). Say that five times every day and it will release indomitable power in your mind.

Your subconscious, which always resents any change, may say to you, "You don't believe any such thing." But remember that your subconscious mind in a sense is one of the greatest liars in existence. It concurs in and sends back to you your own errors about your abilities. You have created the negative attitude in your subconscious and it gives this error back to you. So just turn on your subconscious and say to it, "Now look here, I do believe that. I insist upon believing it." If you talk to your subconscious mind with that positiveness, in due course it will be convinced. One reason is because you are now feeding it positive thoughts. In other words, you are at last telling the truth to your subconscious. After a while your subconscious mind will begin to send back the truth to you, the truth being that with the help of Jesus Christ there isn't any obstacle you cannot overcome.

An effective method for making your subconscious positive in character is to eliminate certain expressions of thought and speech which we may call the "little negatives." These so-called "little negatives" clutter up the average person's conversation, and while each one is seemingly unimportant in itself, the total effect of these attitudes is to condition the mind negatively. When this thought of "little negatives" first occurred to me, I began to analyze my own conversational habits and was shocked by what I found. I discovered that I was making such statements as, "I'm afraid I'll be late," or "I wonder if I'll have a flat tire," or "I don't think I can do that," or "I'll never get through this job. There's so much to do." If something turned out badly, I might say, "Oh, that's just what I expected." Or, again, I might observe a few clouds in the sky and would gloomily state, "I knew it was going to rain."

These are "little negatives" to be sure, and a big thought is of course more powerful than a little one, but it must never be forgotten that "mighty oaks from little acorns grow," and if a mass of "little negatives" clutter up your conversation, they are bound to seep into your mind. It is surprising how they accumulate in force, and presently, before you know it, they will grow into "big negatives." So, I determined to go to work on the "little negatives" and root them out of my conversation. I found that the best way to eliminate them was to deliberately say a positive word about everything.

"If you say you don't want to do, either you don't know how to start, or you don't know what the benefit is." – Swett Marden

When you keep asserting that things are going to work out well, that you can do the job, that you will not have a flat tire, that you will get there on time, by talking up good results you invoke the law of positive effects and good results occur. Things do turn out well. On a roadside billboard I saw an advertisement of a certain brand of motor oil. The slogan read, "A clean engine always delivers power." So will a mind free of negatives produce positives, that is to say, a clean mind will deliver power. Therefore, flush out your thoughts, give yourself a clean mental engine, remembering that a clean mind, even as a clean engine, always delivers power. So, to overcome your obstacles and live the "I don't believe in defeat" philosophy, cultivate a positive-idea pattern deeply in your consciousness. What we do with obstacles is directly determined by our mental attitude. Most of our obstacles, as a matter of fact, are mental in character.

Try Something Than Trying Nothing

A king comes to know that some gold from his palace has been stolen recently. The soldiers find the thief and bring him to the king. He asks angrily: Who gave you the tip to enter my palace? The thief replies: Your minister, and he took his share from me. But the king rejects by saying: You are lying and there is no gold with my minister. The king gives him death punishment and asks his last wish before death.

The thief replies that he wants to show him the trick of flying a horse. The king feels amazed and gives him a horse to fly. The thief, knowing nothing about flying a horse, had succeeded in speculation. Now he asks some time to train the horse and takes a period of three years. The time begins to pass, but in third year something strange happens. A king from different empire attacks his king. And the thief gets free forever.

The Power of Thoughts

Think about certain events in your life, and try to remember what kind of thoughts you thought, before they happened. Try to find the connection between your thoughts and the events. How many times, something happened in your life and you said: "I was sure this was going to happen?" Our predominant thoughts influence our behaviour and attitude, and they, in turn, affect our actions, our life, and the people around us. As our thoughts are, so are our lives. This means that it is of great importance to be careful with our thoughts, especially with thoughts that we often repeat. Thoughts are like a DVD that we play in our mind. What we play, is what we see with our inner eyes, and if we keep playing the same DVD, we will sooner or later create and recreate in our lives. One single thought is not strong enough to make a change, but if the same thought is repeated often, it gradually gains strength. A thought that is often repeated takes root in the subconscious mind, and from there, it affects our lives and even our environment. The great thing about this process is that we don't need to strain or overexert ourselves to make it happen.

"Life is either a daring adventure or nothing." – Helen Keller

All we have to do is to choose a thought that we want to come true, and keep repeating it. Suppose you are shy in the company of people, and you want to change this situation. Forcing yourself to talk with people does not always work, and might make you feel uncomfortable and behave awkwardly. A useful technique is to visualize yourself feeling confident and talking fluently with people. This is similar daydreaming, and is an easy and pleasurable activity. This is a mental activity, which is quite simple and does not require effort.

This is a sort of practical daydreaming, a method of using the power of your thoughts. It is very similar to ordinary daydreaming, yet with some differences. Visualize yourself conversing fluently, with ease and confidence. Imagine how the words just flow from your mouth, how you enjoy expressing yourself, and how everyone pays close attention to every word you say. Build in your mind a perfect scene of whatever you want to accomplish. Put a lot of detail, color, sound, scents and life into these mental scenes. Repeat them often, with faith and attention, and your subconscious mind will accept them as real experiences, and would therefore, assist you in aligning them with your reality in a most natural way. It will make any necessary changes to make your reality fit your mental images.

You can overcome negative habits and build new ones, develop new skills and abilities, and even change your circumstances and attain anything that you truly desire. The power of thoughts can help you get a new job, improve your relationships, earn more money or improve your life. All this does not happen overnight. It needs time, and depends on how sincere you are in your efforts, and on how much time and focus you put into your new way of thinking. This is mental work, but this does not mean that you stay passive and wait for things to happen. You need to keep an open mind and be willing to take action when necessary.

Story – The Egg Seller

Let's talk about an egg seller. His duty was to carry and sell eggs on a bicycle. One day, while riding the bicycle in morning, he hits a wall and all of his eggs get broken. People approach and comment about the dirty smell. Suddenly from the crowd, an uncle appears and says: Leave this matter aside, and think, what will his owner tell him? He will cut money from his salary. So we should do something for him to compensate his loss.

While saying this, the uncle drops ten rupees there with kindness. Now other people also start giving money, and gradually, almost all contribute some amount. After a while, the money becomes more than the eggs' value. The seller collects all the money and prepares to leave the place. But one person appears from behind with a question. He asks: By the way, who is your owner? And the seller replies: The same uncle!

"Don't wrestle with pigs, otherwise you get dirty but he likes." – Swett Marden

A.R Rahman

A.R Rahman is a renowned music director of India.
His Tamil fans affectionately call him – The Musical Storm.
His childhood name was R.S Dileep Kumar.
He was born in 1967 in a middleclass Tamil family of Chennai.
His name A.R Rahman stands for Allah Rakha Rahman.
Rahman is a famous singer, lyricist, and music director.
He follows Sufi Islam religion bestowed in him from his mother.
His parents' names are R.K Shekhar and Kareema Begum.
Rahman began his film career in 1990 with Tamil film 'Roja'.
His father R.K Shekhar was a film score composer.
Rahman assisted his father in the studio playing keyboards.
His father passed away when he was nine years old.
He learnt playing keyboard, piano, harmonium, and guitar.
At the age of eleven, he began playing in orchestra.
He's got Grammy, Academy, BAFTa Awards, and 15 Filmfare Awards.

Thoughts, Feelings and Success

Repeat aloud the word 'success' several times, and notice how you feel. Depending on your mental and emotional makeup, and your mood of the moment, there are two possibilities. You might become inspired, happy and elated, or despondent, unhappy and bitter. In the latter case, you might start telling yourself how miserable you are, and that success is not for you. This may sound strange, but thoughts about success can evoke negative feelings. People who have entertained negative thoughts and feelings most of their lives, expect failure and do not feel worthy of success. If they have experienced lack and hardships, they believe that success is not for them. In these cases, everything associated with success might evoke negative feelings. Your thoughts and feelings can draw or repel success. They shape your beliefs and expectations about success or failure.

Thoughts too often, come and go and change direction like the wind. They influence your mind the same way that the wind affects the direction of a flag. One moment the flag may be fluttering this way, and a moment later in a different direction. One moment you might be thinking one thing or see things from a certain viewpoint, and a moment later this can change. When your thoughts, feelings and moods become steady and under your control, your life also becomes under your control. You become the deciding factor, not the outside influences or passing moods. In order to control your thoughts, feelings and moods and navigate your life, concentration and willpower need to be developed. Concentration and willpower constitute the steering wheel of your life, with which you can navigate the boat of your life toward success and achievement.

"Improve yourself and you will find that the world is less by a rascal." - Thomas Carlyle

Your predominant, habitual thoughts and feelings determine whether you will achieve success or not, and whether you will feel satisfied upon realization or not. This means that you have to be more aware of your thoughts and feelings. It is important to learn to be more positive, less critical, and less worried. Then, when success is achieved, you can enjoy the happiness of achievement. Thoughts, attitudes and habits can be changed. The change does not come overnight. Some inner work is necessary. Positive thoughts and feelings make you happier and more receptive to success, and a positive disposition bestows upon you the ability to enjoy success when it comes. Take it as a challenge, and pay more attention to your thoughts and feelings.

Find out what kind of thoughts you think and what kind of feelings you usually experience in connection with them. If your thoughts and feelings are positive that's okay. However, if you think and feel failure, unhappiness and dissatisfaction, then you need to do something about this. Why is it that people desire success? There is a desire for growth in each one of us. It is the cosmic desire for expression and expansion. This desire manifests in every form of life. We see it everywhere, even in a blade of grass, which can grow on a rock or on a wall. The desire for success is the inner natural desire for growth, expansion and expression.

What is Success?

Success is the realization and achievement of plans, desires or intentions. It is the positive outcome of your actions. It could result in more money, a better job, better relationships, getting a desired object, finding the perfect spouse, attaining fame or power, and the realization of your dreams. Success is not confined to material objects. There is also a mental and a spiritual success, such as getting good grades at school, or making progress with self-improvement or spiritual growth. It is not enough to seek only external success, such as money and possessions. Self-improvement, spiritual growth and inner peace are important too. Without them, you might be successful, but still feel a lack of happiness. People often think that success will bring them the happiness they seek. Sometimes it does, and sometimes it doesn't. Happiness is more dependent on your attitude and inner life and not so much on external conditions.

The Magnetic, Attracting Power of the Mind

The mind attracts certain events, circumstances and people into our lives and repels others. In this respect, it resembles a magnet. Look at the people around you. Some pass through certain events and circumstances, while others pass through different experiences. Some accomplish certain things easily, and others accomplish them with great difficulty or not at all. All this has much to do with the mind. Your mind is composed of the thoughts you think. These thoughts are like magnetic currents. If you keep thinking about some event or action, it might become a part of your life.

"Men are born mad but some remain so." – Samuel Beckett

This holds true when thinking about things you want and about things that you don't want. You attract into your life what you think about frequently. It does not mean that every thought gets materialized. Most of the thoughts are either not repeated long enough to gain sufficient strength, or you might also think contradictory thoughts, or you might have doubts about what you are thinking. Thoughts that lack strength and focus are like a weak magnet; they hardly have any attractive power.

You have seen how a magnet draws metal objects. You know how one thing attracts another. This is a natural phenomenon that you have to believe in. A strong and big magnet draws bigger objects than a small and weak one. Magnets have another peculiar characteristic. One side of the magnet draws, and the other side repels. The magnet draws to itself everything made of iron, useful objects or just junk. The mind acts in the same way. It attracts into your life positive and negative situations and events, according to the thoughts that you think. Like the magnet, the mind not only attracts, but also repels. If you do not believe you can get or accomplish something, then you repel it. So you need to generate a belief about success in yourself either by reading about success, meeting successful people or dreaming about success in open eyes.

Thoughts of lack, doubts and fears create a repellent force. This negative thinking creating more negativity in your mind. So you need to cure your negative thinking before it creates another negativity. It is as if you are creating a wind that blows away what you want. In this way, you prevent what you want from reaching you. There are several ways to charge your mind and thoughts with magnetic power. A strong desire, concentration and faith are a few of the important ingredients for infusing power into thoughts. We often activate the magnetic power of their mind unconsciously, without knowing what we are doing. When we know the rules, we become able to activate the magnetic power of the mind consciously, positively and effectively.

Sudha Chandran

Sudha Chandran is a Bharatanatyam dancer and actress.
She was born in 1965 in a Tamil family in Mumbai.
Her father K.D Chandran was an actor in Mumbai.
When she was eighteen, she lost her right leg in an accident.
Sudha however continued dancing and got established.
She is known for her role of Ramola Sikand in Kahin Kisi Roz.
Chandran did M.A in economics from Mithibai College, Mumbai.
She started acting for Telugu film Mayuri based on her life.
The film was remade in Hindi as Naache Mayuri.
Sudha got two awards for her role in Mayuri.
She is given an honorary doctorate degree by Bareily University.
Sudha Chandran married assistant director Ravi Dang.
Her biography is a part of education for school children.

"Success doesn't come by memorizing principles but applying them." – Osho

Mania, Disorder and Complex

Mania, also known as manic syndrome, is a mental and behavioural problem defined as a state of abnormally elevated arousal, affect, and energy level, or a state of heightened overall activation. It may also be with enhanced affective expression. During a manic episode, an individual will experience rapidly changing emotions and moods, highly influenced by surrounding stimuli. Although mania is often conceived as a "mirror image" to depression, the heightened mood can be either euphoric or dysphonic. As the mania intensifies, irritability can be more pronounced and result in anxiety or anger.

1. Hypermania: Intensity and disorientation in oneself.
2. Logomania: Excessive desire of talking.
3. Dipsomania: Too much attachment with alcohol.
4. Dromomania: Excessing desire of traveling.
5. Erotomania: Excessive sexual desire.
6. Mythomania: Persistent habit of lying.
7. Oniomania: Excessive interest in shopping.

Disorder is referred as mental disorder. It is a disease of particular abnormal condition of mind and is not immediately due to any external injury. Disorders are health conditions involving changes in emotion, thinking or behaviour or a combination of these). Mental illnesses can be associated with distress or problems functioning in social, work or family activities.

1. Bipolar disorder: A mood disorder for a period of time.
2. Personality disorder: Disruptive patterns of thinking.
3. Anxiety disorder: Excessive fear of perceived threats.
4. Schizophrenia: Disturbance in thoughts, feeling and behaviour.
5. Trauma disorder: Post-traumatic stress problem.

Complex or mental complex is defined as a group or system of related ideas or impulses that have a common emotional tone and exert a strong but usually unconscious influence on the individual's attitudes and behaviour. This means that complexes comprise core patterns of desires, emotions, memories and perceptions that unknowingly influence the way a person thinks and behaves.

1. Inferiority complex: Feeling that you are not good enough in life.
2. Superiority complex: Feeling that you are better than all else.
3. Persecution complex: An irrational fear you are being ill-treated.
4. Oedipus complex: A deep affection for the parent.
5. Don Juan complex: Men who view women as a source of pleasure.

"If you can't fight for justice, you will die in crime." Niranjan Jha Showman

Chapter 7

Feelings, Emotions and Creative Visualization

You have probably heard or read about creative visualization. Maybe, you have tried it. The idea is that by visualizing a mental image of a desired object or situation, you can attract it into your life. In this way, you can shape your life, behaviour and circumstances. To make this power work, visualization is important, but is not enough. Some additional ingredients are required to energize the thoughts into action. These ingredients are desire and emotions.

What makes you take action, a cold uninteresting thought, or one charged with emotion? When you listen to a lecture, which lecturer rivets your attention, someone who talks in a boring, listless manner, or a lecturer who talks with zest and emotion? When you meet a total stranger for the first time, who leaves a stronger impression on you, a cold, dull person, or one full of energy and enthusiasm? People, actions and thoughts charged with emotion make a stronger impact. Thoughts that are charged with emotional energy are the ones that affect you more, and drive you into action. Feelings and emotions energize your thoughts and fill them with power.

Emotions and feelings energize thoughts, the same way that electricity makes electric instruments work. The best instrument won't function without electricity. In order for a thought to act and manifest, it needs something to give it life and energy. Feelings and emotions are this something. If your desire is strong, then you can generate the necessary emotional energy. However, sometimes, the emotional power you produce is not enough to make things happen. In these cases, you need, in some way, to strengthen your emotional energy. It is possible to produce emotional energy when you need this power. It is like connecting a television or a radio to a wall socket in order to let the electricity flow. You do so by producing positive and happy feelings of success and satisfaction, and associating them with your desire. Everyone has, at least a few times, experienced some sort of success. Remember and visualize any success you have achieved in the past. Even small manifestations of success count.

In your mind, relive successful events, such as getting good grades, receiving a compliment from someone whose opinion you value, finding a good job, getting a promotion or achieving success associated with your work or business. You may choose any event from the past. Relive the event of success in your imagination, visualize it as clearly as possible, and let the positive and happy feelings, which you experienced at that time, become alive again. When these feelings are aroused, it is time to think about your current goal. Live and experience these feelings and emotions in your imagination, and associate them with your present goal. This action, will inject energy into your thoughts and make them powerful. When your thoughts are charged with emotional power they are transmitted to the surrounding environment. They are even picked up by other people, who will consequently help you to bring your thoughts into reality. Thoughts evoke feelings, and feelings evoke thoughts.

"You are a real brave if you win the conflicts of life." Aristotle

Story – Let the Game Get Going

A young boy enters a salon and the barber whispers to his customer: This is the dumbest kid in the world. Watch while I prove it to you. The barber puts a dollar bill in one hand and two quarters in the other, then he calls the boy over and asks: Which do you we want, son? The boy takes the quarters and leaves. The customer sees that the barber was right.

Later, when the customer leaves the salon, he sees the same young boy coming out of the ice cream store. He says: Hey, son! May I ask you a question? Why did you take the quarters instead of the dollar bill? The boy licks his cone and replies: Because the day I take the dollar, the game is over! So, let the game get going.

The Restless Mind

Most of our body's functions are automatic activities. Take for example, breathing. We constantly breathe, but we hardly pay this function any attention. The blood moves automatically through the veins, but we are hardly aware of its movement. So it is with many other bodily functions. Thinking is also, to a large extent, an automatic continuous activity. Thoughts come and go incessantly from morning till night. There is no rest from them for a moment. Most of these thoughts are not exactly invited; they just come, occupy the attention for a while, and then disappear.

Our inner consciousness is like the sky, and our thoughts are like clouds. The clouds drift through the sky, hide it for a while, and then disappear. They are not permanent. So are our thoughts. They hide our inner self, our sense of being. When on thought goes, another thought comes, and we always find ourselves thinking, never paying attention to what lies beyond our thoughts. Thoughts resemble the waves of the ocean, which are always in a state of motion, never standing still. The mind, which attracts and produces thoughts, finds it hard to stand still. It always thinks about whatever it sees. It likes to compare, analyze, reason, and to ask questions. It never stops or rests, even for a short while.

Everyone's mind automatically accepts certain thoughts, but filters out and rejects others. This is the reason why some people occupy their minds with thoughts about a certain subject, while others don't even think about this same subject. It seems as if everyone possesses a different mental filter. Why some people are attracted to football and others don't? Why some love and admire a certain singer and others don't? Why some people think a lot about a certain subject, and other never think about it? It is all due to this inner filter. This is an automatic and unconscious filter. Do you consciously tell certain thoughts to come and tell others to go away? This is usually an automatic activity. This filter has been shaped according to the influences that have affected you since childhood.

"There is no light unless you burn yourself." – Thomas S. Monson

Every event, occurrence, word or suggestion has an affect on the mind, which produces thoughts accordingly. The mind is like a thought factory, working in shifts, day and night, producing thoughts. Everyone is thinking and producing thoughts. It is as if we are living in an ocean of thoughts. We constantly pick one, let it pass through our minds and then pick up another one. It is like catching a fish from the ocean, throwing it again into the water and catching another one. We spend a lot of energy and time thinking about unimportant, and mostly negative passing thoughts. Why let thoughts rule the mind, instead of being their master? Why not enjoy inner peace, and choose only beneficial and desirable thoughts? Why let your thoughts treat you like a relentless boss that constantly gives you an errand after errand to do? There is no freedom here. It is freedom when you can choose your thoughts. It is freedom, when you are able to decide which thought to accept, and which one to reject.

Galileo Galilei

Galileo Galilei was born in 1564 in Pisa, Italy.
He is regarded as the father of physics.
In his childhood, his family moved to Florence for better lifestyle.
He studied mathematics and astronomy and became a math's professor.
He is also known as a mathematician, astronomer and philosopher.
Without marriage, with Marina, he had two daughters and one son.
His achievement includes the improvement to the telescope.
On his statement: The sun is the center of universe, he faced criticism.
He also said: The scripture is a book of poetry and songs, not instructions.
Later the Catholic Church condemned his views publically.
The church arrested him and ordered in-house captivity for lifetime.
During his 70's, he went blind a developed lots of physical complications.
Recently the pope accepted the mistake committed by the church.
The Vatican proposed erect a statue of him inside the walls.
He died in 1642 in Florence at the age of 77.

Peace of Mind

Do you desire to enjoy peace of mind? Do you want to be able to stay calm and relaxed in difficult and trying situations? It is not as difficult as it might seem. I meet people who say that they desire peace of mind, but how can they get it, if they never do anything to attain it? In a world full of tension, conflict and competition, peace of mind is a great necessity. A person, who possesses peace of mind is able to remain calm, peaceful and unaffected by outside events. This peace has nothing to do with indifference or laziness. In fact, you can be peaceful, yet energetic, enterprising and possessing a sharp and keen mind.

"If the blind leads the blind, both will fall into the ditch." – Plato

Meditation, concentration exercises, guided imagination, affirmations and breathing exercises are a few of the techniques that lead to peace of mind. Every one of these techniques will gradually make your mind more calm and peaceful. As you go on with your chosen technique, your level of inner peace will rise. You will experience it not only while using one of the above mentioned techniques, but at other times too. You will discover that as by-product, you also gain inner happiness and inner strength, discipline, better judgment and stronger mental powers. When your mind is peaceful, it unconsciously radiates peace to the people who happen to be around you.

When you can switch off your thoughts, your mind becomes peaceful, happier, and more focused. You might say that you don't have the time to work on gaining peace of mind, but the truth is that you can always find the time, if you really desire it. You might believe that peace of mind can be gained only under special conditions and in special places. That is not true. Circumstances should not bar your way. If your desire for peace of mind is strong enough, you can attain it whether you live in an ashram or in a noisy city. Peace of mind can be yours, if you make the effort to relax and calm down your mind. Try this exercise:

1) Sit down comfortably.
2) Go through your body from the head to your toes.
3) Relax every tense muscle.
4) Take a few deep breaths.
5) Now think about something that inspires you or makes you happy.
6) Enjoy the happiness and calmness that you are experiencing.

You need to repeat this procedure whenever you feel tense and nervous. This is only the first step. Peace of mind is gained through various methods, but especially by concentration and meditation practiced on a regular basis.

Netflix
Netflix is an over-the-top video platform.
It also works as a film production company.
Netflix has headquarter in Los Gatos, California, USA.
It was founded in 1997 by Reed Hastings and Marc Randolph.
In 2021, Netflix had 209 million subscribers worldwide.
This company's starting business was selling and renting DVDs.
Netflix introduced streaming media in 2007 much before Amazon.
This company also entered in content production with their associates.
Its first video show is – House of Cards.
Netflix released 126 series and films in 2016.
In 2020, Netflix became the largest entertainment company.
The show 'Red Notice' is the most successful Netflix movie.

"A wise can pretend to be stupid but a stupid can't pretend to be wise." – Socrates

Inner Peace and Outer Peace

Real peace comes from the inside, and is not dependent on outside conditions. Inner peace is a state, in which the mind becomes calm and tranquil, and thoughts are controlled and disciplined. Ordinarily, the mind is in a state of incessant thinking. Thoughts come and go every hour of the day. Many of these thoughts are about unimportant matters, or are negative thoughts, worries and fears. The mind keeps asking questions, comparing, analyzing, commenting on everything, chattering and not allowing any moment of rest. This state of affairs is one of the reasons for the craving for inner peace. Yet, though there is longing for peace of mind, most people continue to let restless thoughts and worries fill their minds, thus keeping inner peace away. Inner peace appears, when the flow of thoughts subsides. Only when your mind becomes tranquil you can enjoy inner peace. Only when you make peace inside, within yourself, does real peace come into being in your outside world.

When a storm is raging, the waves toss a boat up and down, from one wave to another. Only when the storm and waves cease, can the boat sail smoothly. So it is with peace of mind. You experience it, only after the winds and gales of the mind and thoughts calm down. If the inner world is in peace, then the outer circumstances begin to reflect this inner peace. Outer peace always follows inner peace. A peaceful mind broadcasts peace and affects the surrounding environment. Anyone who comes in contact with a peaceful person, senses this peace, and unconsciously, responds and behaves accordingly.

What happens, if you talk calmly with someone who is angry, or who is talking in a loud voice? Sooner or later he will lower his voice. What happens, if you keep calm and tranquil in situations that make other people nervous or restless? You act efficiently, and make fewer errors.   These are just a few examples of the effect inner peace has on the outside world. You can attain inner peace mainly through concentration, meditation and yoga. The keys to inner peace are the ability to calm down the mind, reduce its restlessness, and free it from the compulsion of constant and restless thinking and worrying.

If you work on your mind and emotions you can achieve inner peace, and consequently, enjoy outer peace. It does not matter what are your external conditions and what is the state of affairs around you. If you work toward inner peace, your life and circumstances will change to reflect your inner peace. Experiences of inner peace are not as rare as you might think, but they are often only temporary. They occur when you are absorbed in an interesting activity, like watching an interesting movie, reading a book or watching a beautiful landscape. They usually last for a short time, until the mind becomes active again. A good example of temporary inner peace is a vacation, when you are away from home. After a day or two you begin to experience some kind of inner calmness and tranquillity. The mind's feverish tendency to think is quelled down, and the level of worries and endless thinking drops down. In this state of mind, you feel more relaxed and happy, and therefore, you enjoy your vacation.

"Learning should be followed by practicing and practicing should be followed by applying." – Niranjan Jha Showman

By the way, have you noticed that people, who are on vacation, are usually more patient, friendly and well-disposed to everyone? This is because their minds are more peaceful. Temporary inner peace is fine, but not enough. In order to experience peace more often and more deeply, and independently of outer conditions, you need to undergo inner training. It is possible to enjoy the same peace and happiness that you have experienced on your vacations, even while working, carrying your duties, at home or while with people. This state, can be reached through concentration, meditation, yoga and a few other means. Nowadays there are so many opportunities for inner work. There are teachers, books, workshops, courses, and of course the Internet. There is no lack of information and guidance. However, it is you, who have to decide that inner and outer peace is one of your priorities, and begin doing something to attain it.

Charlie Chaplin

Charlie Chaplin was a famous comedian of the world.
He was born in 1889 in London, England.
Charlie's parents were music hall entertainers in London.
Charlie spent childhood in poverty at Walworth, South London.
He was sent to work at the age of seven, but later joined a school.
When he was nine, his mother fell into mental disorder.
Through father's contact, Charlie joined a dancing group.
At the age of thirteen, he abandoned education and became an actor.
Within five years, Chaplin became a famous comedy performer.
He was invited to join New York Motion Pictures Company.
Charlie rose to fame by performing in several movies of silent era.
He married four times and had eleven children.
Charlie Chaplin died in 1977 in Switzerland.

The Power of Concentration

Concentration is the ability to focus mind on one single object or thought to the exclusion of everything else. It is the ability to hold attention focused on what you are doing. Doing one thing, and at the same time thinking of something else, shows lack of concentration. This might lead to making mistakes and to lack of efficiency. Few possess really strong powers of concentration. Most people recognize its importance, but few do something to develop or strengthen it. Concentration has great value. It helps you to do your work more efficiently. It strengthens the memory, makes it easier and faster to study, and makes you more conscious and aware of your surroundings. Actions, tasks and work are performed better, faster and with fewer errors.

"One who is inactive in bringing improvement to their nation is a half terrorist." – Niranjan Jha Showman

Concentration is required for creative visualization, affirmations and psychic powers, and is of major importance for practicing meditation. It helps you to control the incessant flow of your thoughts, and thereby, bring peace of mind and freedom from nagging thoughts. As the ability to concentrate grows, fewer thoughts are able to intrude into the mind without permission. This means more mental mastery and more inner peace and happiness.

It is important to possess good powers of concentration, if you wish to conduct your daily affairs of life in an efficient and effective way, to succeed in the material world or to grow spiritually. Concentration can be improved and strengthened by proper exercises, just like developing and strengthening the physical muscles through bodybuilding exercises. If you lift weights, you strengthen the muscles of your body. If you perform concentration exercises you strengthen your mental muscles. Concentration is a simple process, though not so easy to practice. This is because the mind is very much accustomed to running here and there, and resists any effort that aims to control and calm it down. Yet, by proper exercises it is possible to train the mind and teach it to focus exclusively on one subject or object at a time. The more time you devote to training and exercising your mind, and the more sincerely you practice the exercises, the stronger your concentration would become.

Developing Willpower and Self Discipline

Most people admire and respect strong individuals, who have won great success by manifesting willpower and self-discipline. They admire people, who improved their life, learned new skills, overcame difficulties and hardships or rose high in their chosen field. The truth is that everyone can reach high levels of willpower and self- discipline, through a practical method of training. These skills are not reserved for a few special people.

Willpower and self-discipline are two of the most important and useful inner powers in everyone's life, and have always been considered as essential tools for success in all areas of life. They can be learned and developed like any other skill, yet, in spite of this, only few take any steps to develop and strengthen them in a systematic way. What is willpower? It is the inner strength that makes it possible to make a decision and follow it through, take action, and handle and execute any aim or task until it is accomplished, regardless of inner and outer resistance, discomfort or difficulties. Willpower bestows the ability to overcome laziness, temptations and negative habits, and to carry out actions, even if they require effort, are unpleasant and tedious, or are contrary to one's habits.

One of the most simple and effective methods for strengthening willpower and self-discipline is by refusing to satisfy unimportant and unnecessary desires. Everyone is constantly confronted and tempted by an endless stream of desires and distractions, many of which are not really important, useful or of any real value.

"Character without courage is ineffective, courage without character is oppression." – Shiv Khera

By learning to refuse to satisfy every one of them, you get stronger. Rejecting, and refusing to satisfy useless, harmful or unnecessary desires and actions, sharpen and strengthen your inner strength. By constant practice, your inner power grows, just like exercising your muscles at a gym increases your physical strength. In both cases, when you need inner power or physical strength, they are available at your disposal.

Story – The Earth is Round

Once there was a king in a territory who was very generous to the public. Learning about his prominence, a hermit comes to his court with an immortalizing apple. He gives the apple to the king telling him that that will make him immortal. But the king adored his queen tremendously, so he gives the apple to her considering her worthy to live forever. However the queen had a lover, so she thought he should live forever instead of her.

And she happily gives the same fruit to him as a gift from her side. But then the lover visited a prostitute, so he gives the apple to her against some dues that he was unable to pay. Now the prostitute, looking at the apple in hand, doesn't feel worthy to live same life eternally. She thinks her king is the right person to eat this apple and be immortal. Next day, the prostitute comes to the king's court and gives the same apple to him.

The Power of Repeated Words and Thoughts

Thinking is usually a mixture of words, sentences, mental images and sensations. Thoughts are visitors, who visit the central station of the mind. They come, stay a while, and then disappear, making space for other thoughts. Some of these thoughts stay longer, gain power, and affect the life of the person thinking them. Most people, allow thoughts connected with worries, fears, anger or unhappiness occupy their mind most of the time. They keep engaging their minds with inner conversation about negative situations and actions.

This inner conversation eventually affects the subconscious mind, making it accept and take seriously the thoughts and ideas expressed in those inner conversations. It is of vital importance to be careful of what goes into the subconscious mind. Words and thoughts that are repeated often get stronger by the repetitions, sink into the subconscious mind and affect the behavior, actions and reactions of the person involved. The subconscious mind regards the words and thoughts that get lodged inside it as expressing and describing a real situation, and therefore, endeavors to align the words and thoughts with reality. It works diligently to make these words and thoughts a reality in the life of the person saying or thinking them.

"Some make things happen, some watch things happen, some just wander and ask - what happened." – David Hume

The thoughts that you express through your words shape your life. This is often done unconsciously. Most people don't pay special attention to their thoughts and the words they use, often allowing outside conditions and circumstances determine what they think about. They let the outside world affects their inner world. They let the outside world determine what they think about. If you consciously, choose the thoughts, phrases and words that you repeat in your mind, your life will start to change. You will begin creating new situations and circumstances. You will be using the power of affirmations. Affirmations are sentences that are repeated often, stating a particular desire or goal. These sentences, sink into the subconscious mind, which in turn, releases its enormous power to materialize the intention of them. This does not mean that every word you utter will bring results. In order to trigger the subconscious mind into action, the affirmation has to be said with attention, intention and with feeling, and to be phrased in positive words results. Consider the following two sentences:

1. I am not weak anymore.
2. I am strong and powerful.

Though both sentences express the same idea, but in different words, the first one is a negative sentence. It creates in the mind a mental image of weakness. This is wrong wording. The second sentence awakens in the mind a mental image of strength. Sometimes, the results might be fast, but often, depending on your goal, results take time to appear, which means you need to persist with repeating the affirmations. It is not enough to repeat an affirmation a few times and expect your life to change. It is important to choose the right affirmation for the specific situation. You also need to feel comfortable with the words you repeat, so as not to awaken inner resistance.

Charles Babbage

Charles Babbage is regarded as the father of computer.
He was born in 1791 at Walworth Road, London.
His father Benjamin Babbage was a banking partner.
Charles couldn't attend schools because of his mental illness.
His parents arranged tutors for his education.
He studied mathematics deeply and became a professor in Cambridge.
Babbage won gold medal for teaching at Cambridge University.
His father, wife and son, all died in 1827.
These deaths caused him to go into mental breakdown.
Charles sought a method of calculating tables without human errors.
Babbage invented the machine in 1822 and named Analytical Engine.
Charles Babbage died in 1871 at Marylebone, London.
His half brain is kept at Hunterian Museum in Royal College.
And the other half is in Science Museum of London.

"Experience is the name of calamity you have overcome." – Emerson

Things to Learn in Life

1. Spend Time with Family
There is nothing in this world like the support of your family. Your parents, wife or children can be your support systems if you choose to make them so. Do not push them away when trouble brews in your head. Share concerns with whosoever you feel close to.

2. Don't Shun Your Friends
While you can always set the fair-weather kinds apart, your genuine friends are most likely to offer companionship and perhaps an ear, when you need it the most. Even if you do not feel like talking, hanging out with the boys can give you a feeling of companionship.

3. Do Social Work
There is no better remedy to inner turmoil than serving others. Try and spend some time after or before work, or on weekends, with special children, underprivileged children or physically handicapped children. If you are an animal lover, you can do voluntary work at a shelter. Giving without expectations can do wonders for your mind and soul. The sensibility of the suffering of the rest of the world also helps lessen one's own dilemma to a certain extent.

4. Exercise
Hit the gym. Go for an early morning jog. Make swimming every evening, or at least thrice a week, a habit. Once your body feels energised, so will your mind, helping throw feelings of loneliness out of the window.

The above remedies can help curb the situation of being lonely to a great extent, if practiced diligently. However, if you still feel incapable of handling the matter yourself, consult a professional and get your life back on track. At war with your mind, wondering how to offload the plethora of thoughts that keep plaguing you all day long? Well, yes, such thoughts are likely to cause much distress when you are trying to study, or work or even sleep. No matter how hard you are trying to concentrate, your mind refuses to calm down. Do you suffer these symptoms? Are you wondering how to keep it under control, and how to calm your overactive mind? The easiest way to calm your thoughts is reading your favourite book, listen to your favourite song or play your favourite movie. You can even try those silly games you used to play as a kid, such as standing in front of a table fan and listening to your robotic voice!

Fantasising might make your brain work harder, even though the purpose is exactly the opposite, but then, who is complaining? You can fantasise about being at your dream destination, driving your favourite sports car or bike, or spending some intimate moments with the neighbours next door! Look at your wall clock and start observing the movement of its hands. It might not make any kind of sense whatsoever and it might be boring as hell, but that's precisely the point. The lesser sense it makes the lesser work your senses do, literally!

"A really talented person can't live without doing what he can." – Epicurus

Story – The Doctor's Skill

There was a doctor in a town. He puts a signboard stating: Get yourself cured from any disease for 500 rupees or take 1000 rupees back. A patient comes in and says: I have lost taste of my tongue. The doctor orders the nurse: Open 'Box 22' and give him four drops. The patient blurts out: It is petrol. The doctor responds fervently: You got your taste back, so pay 500 rupees. The patient goes out after paying, but he cultivates another plan. Next day again he comes complaining about another disease.

This time he reports having weak memory. The doctor orders the nurse again: Open 'Box 22' and…. The patient resists: But that is for taste. The doctor replies: You got your memory back, so pay 500 rupees. Next day again he comes complaining about weak eyesight. The doctor says: We have no cure for this, and you can take 1000 rupees. But while giving him money, he gives him only 500, on which, the patient reacts: It is 500. The doctor replies: You got your eyesight back, now pay 500 rupees.

Coca-Cola

Coca-Cola or Coke is a soft drink by Coca-Cola Company.
It was invented as a non-alcoholic drink in nineteenth century.
John Pemberton of Atlanta, Georgia invented this drink.
Coca means 'coca leaves' and cola means 'kola nuts'.
There two ingredients are also used in caffeine.
Caffeine is a psychoactive stimulant available in coffee.
The current formula of Coca-Cola is a close secret.
It is the world's sixth most valuable brand.
This soft drink is sold in two hundred countries worldwide.
Coca-Cola also received Best Bottling Company award.
Its logo was designed by Frank Robinson in 1885.
Coca-Cola is a global symbol of American tastes.
Coke doesn't sell only drink but also happiness.

Learn to Focus

Yes, the focus still remains a problem, but not yours! Focusing on another's dilemma is bound to make you divert your energy away from the pile of rubbish weighing your mind down. What's more, you might just be doing your buddy a huge favour by being his friend in need. Exercising is much more than keeping you physically fit. A jog in the park every morning rejuvenates your brain and the whole thought process. Feel yourself more filled with energy than ever before!

"There is a difference between play to win and play not to lose." – Shiv Khera

What is self-discipline? It is the ability to reject instant gratification, in order to gain something better. It manifests as perseverance and the ability to stick to actions, thoughts and behavior, which lead to improvement and success, despite obstacles or difficulties. It also manifests. Both of willpower and self-discipline are essential for daily activities and decisions, and also for making major decisions and attaining major success. They are required for doing a good job, for studying, building a business, losing weight, bodybuilding, maintaining good relationships, changing habits, self-improvement, meditation, spiritual growth, keeping and carrying out promises, and for almost everything else.

Chapter 8

Maintain Your Health

Nine Requisites for Contended Living;

HEALTH is enough to make work a pleasure.
WEALTH is enough to support your needs.
STRENGTH is to battle with difficulties and overcome them.
GRACE is enough to confess your sins and forsake them.
PATIENCE is enough to toil until some good is accomplished.
CHARITY is enough to see some good in your neighbour.
LOVE is enough to move you to be useful and helpful to others.
FAITH is enough to make real the things of God.
HOPE is enough to remove all anxious fears concerning the future.

People who are unable to motivate themselves must be content with mediocrity, no matter how impressive their other talents. While Marilyn Monroe's star burned out early, she did have a period of great success in her life. Despite a rough upbringing and being told by modelling agents that she should instead consider being a secretary, Monroe became a pin-up, model and actress that still strikes a chord with people today.

Oliver Stone, this Oscar-winning filmmaker began his first novel while at Yale, a project that eventually caused him to fail out of school. This would turn out to be a poor decision as the text was rejected by publishers and was not published until 1998, at which time it was not well-received. After dropping out of school, Stone moved to Vietnam to teach English, later enlisting in the army and fighting in the war, a battle that earning two Purple Hearts and helped him find the inspiration for his later work that often centre around war.

"It is better being scolded by wise than praised by foolish." – Proverb

Christopher Columbus

Christopher Columbus is regarded as the discoverer of America.
He was born in 1451 in the city of Genoa, Italy (then Spain).
He spent childhood working at his family's cheese shop.
Then he worked on a ship to support the king in warfare.
Christopher married Filipa who was Portugal governor's daughter.
From 1482, he started trading along the coasts of West Africa.
After his wife's death, he found a mistress in Spain to live with.
He studied Latin, Portuguese, astronomy, geography, history and Bibile
Columbus estimated westward route shorter for Asia for spice trading.
Spanish queen Isabella supported his voyage and exploration.
His proposal was a matter of disbelief as it was impossible to return alive.
Columbus departed from Spain with 3 ships for 5 weeks' of voyage.
Assuming East Asia, he reached Bahamas' island which he named San Salvador.
Columbus mistook it for India and referred to the inhabitants as Indians.
After seven months he returned to Spain with 9 natives alive.
At death in 1506 also he was convinced that he had voyaged to Asia.

Magnetic, Attracting Power of Mind

The mind attracts certain events, circumstances and people into our lives and repels others. In this respect, it resembles a magnet. Look at the people around you. Some pass through certain events and circumstances, while others pass through different experiences. Some accomplish certain things easily, and others accomplish them with great difficulty or not at all. All this has much to do with the mind. Your mind is composed of the thoughts you think. These thoughts are like magnetic currents. If you keep thinking about some event or action, it might become a part of your life. This holds true when thinking about things you want and about things that you don't want. You attract into your life what you think about frequently. It does not mean that every thought gets materialized. Most of the thoughts are either not repeated long enough to gain sufficient strength, or you might also think contradictory thoughts, or you might have doubts about what you are thinking.

Thoughts that lack strength and focus are like a weak magnet; they hardly have any attractive power. You have seen how a magnet draws metal objects. A strong and big magnet draws bigger objects than a small and weak one. Magnets have another peculiar characteristic. One side of the magnet draws, and the other side repels. The magnet draws to itself everything made of iron, useful objects or just junk. The mind acts in the same way. It attracts into your life positive and negative situations and events, according to the thoughts that you think. Like the magnet, the mind not only attracts, but also repels. If you do not believe you can get or accomplish something, then you repel it.

"Be obedient to your superior and your inferior will obey you." – Dale Carnegie

Thoughts of lack, doubts and fears create a repellent force. It is as if you are creating a wind that blows away what you want. In this way, you prevent what you want from reaching you. There are several ways to charge your mind and thoughts with magnetic power. A strong desire, concentration and faith are a few of the important ingredients for infusing power into thoughts. We often activate the magnetic power of their mind unconsciously, without knowing what we are doing. When we know the rules, we become able to activate the magnetic power of the mind consciously, positively and effectively.

When you think, you broadcast your thoughts, affecting the minds of other people, and attracting to you people, who think along the same lines as you do, and can therefore, help you with your plans and goals. This process also heightens your awareness and perceptiveness of any opportunity that might come your way, connected with your thoughts. Why not become conscious of your thoughts, choose to think the ones that are beneficial to you, and consciously and advantageously utilize the power of attraction of your thoughts? Remember, what you think about intently, with attention and feeling, is attracted to you. It might be something material or non-material. The power of attraction is a universal power and manifests everywhere and in everything. It is the power that holds the Universe together. Without it there would not be any world.

You have probably heard or read about creative visualization. Maybe, you have tried it. The idea is that by visualizing a mental image of a desired object or situation, you can attract it into your life. In this way, you can shape your life, behaviour and circumstances. To make this power work, visualization is important, but is not enough. Some additional ingredients are required to energize the thoughts into action. These ingredients are desire and emotions. What makes you take action, a cold uninteresting thought, or one charged with emotion? When you listen to a lecture, which lecturer rivets your attention, someone who talks in a boring, listless manner, or a lecturer who talks with zest and emotion? When you meet a total stranger for the first time, who leaves a stronger impression on you, a cold, dull person, or one full of energy and enthusiasm?

People, actions and thoughts charged with emotion make a stronger impact. Thoughts that are charged with emotional energy are the ones that affect you more, and drive you into action. Feelings and emotions energize your thoughts and fill them with power. Emotions and feelings energize thoughts, the same way that electricity makes electric instruments work. The best instrument won't function without electricity. In order for a thought to act and manifest, it needs something to give it life and energy. Feelings and emotions are this something. If your desire is strong, then you can generate the necessary emotional energy. However, sometimes, the emotional power you produce is not enough to make things happen. In these cases, you need, in some way, to strengthen your emotional energy. It is possible to produce emotional energy when you need this power. It is like connecting a television or a radio to a wall socket in order to let the electricity flow.

"A really intelligent man feels what others only know." – Robert Arrington

You do so by producing positive and happy feelings of success and satisfaction, and associating them with your desire. Everyone has, at least a few times, experienced some sort of success. Remember and visualize any success you have achieved in the past. Even small manifestations of success count. In your mind, relive successful events, such as getting good grades, receiving a compliment from someone whose opinion you value, finding a good job, getting a promotion or achieving success associated with your work or business. You may choose any event from the past. Relive the event of success in your imagination, visualize it as clearly as possible, and let the positive and happy feelings, which you experienced at that time, become alive again. When these feelings are aroused, it is time to think about your current goal. Live and experience these feelings and emotions in your imagination, and associate them with your present goal. This action, will inject energy into your thoughts and make them powerful. When your thoughts are charged with emotional power they are transmitted to the surrounding environment.

They are even picked up by other people, who will consequently help you to bring your thoughts into reality. Thoughts evoke feelings, and feelings evoke thoughts. Our habitual thoughts influence the way we feel, and our feelings influence the way we think. There is always an interaction between thoughts and feelings. Learning to take advantage of the combined power of thoughts and feelings can take you a long way toward achieving your goals. When you think, you broadcast your thoughts, affecting the minds of other people, and attracting to you people, who think along the same lines as you do, and can therefore, help you with your plans and goals. This process also heightens your awareness and perceptiveness of any opportunity that might come your way, connected with your thoughts.

Michael Jackson

Michael Jackson is regarded as the best pop music entertainer of all time.
He is was a singer, dancer, musician and also lyricist and philanthropist.
He was born in 1958 in an Afro-American labor family of Indiana.
He had 10 siblings and he received extreme stress of poverty.
His father used to beat and abuse him of having a fat nose.
At the age of 6, he joined a small music band as a backup musician.
He grew up performing backup vocals and dancing.
At the age of 8, he began lead vocals in striptease adult dance.
In 1980, he became the king of pop music, rock, funk, jack swing, and disco.
He had multiple Grammy Awards, American Music Awards, and World Records,
He married twice and was supporting 39 charities
Up to 45 years, he remained a dominant figure in music sensation.
He was invited to the White House to receive award from President Reagan.
In house, he had Ferris wheel, theatre, and 40 patrolling guards.
He died in 2009 in his bed at Los Angeles.

"Courage is not absence of fear but overcoming fear." – Dante

Personality Improvement

If knowledge is there, I'll get it. If diligence is there, I'll do it. If perseverance is there, I'll maintain it. And, if success is there, I'll achieve it. Real peace comes from the inside, and is not dependent on outside conditions. Inner peace is a state, in which the mind becomes calm and tranquil, and thoughts are controlled and disciplined. Ordinarily, the mind is in a state of incessant thinking. Thoughts come and go every hour of the day. Many of these thoughts are about unimportant matters, or are negative thoughts, worries and fears.

To improve your personality, you need to focus on these points:

1. Overcoming depression
2. Understanding smile effects
3. Killing inertia
4. Art of self-motivation
5. Believing in the Supreme
6. Health and mind
7. Fighting disorders
8. Growing self-persona
9. Win-win attitude
10. Be a good leader
11. Be a good speaker
12. Believe in prosperity as essence of life.

Bruce Lee

Bruce Lee is regarded as the most prominent martial artist of all time.
He was a Hong Kong and American popular figure.
He was also an actor, director, producer, and philosopher.
He was considered a pop culture icon of 20th century.
Bruce Lee bridged the gap between East World and West World.
He changed the way Asians were presented in American films.
Lee was born in 1940 in San Francisco, America.
Lee had the citizenship of the US and Hong Kong.
His parents performed as opera actors in Hong Kong.
He acted as a child artist and later learnt and performed martial art.
He took admission in Washington University and also continued martial art.
Bruce Lee won six awards as a martial artist actor.
In 1973, Bruce Lee collapsed to death in a film studio.

"I count him braver who overcomes his desires than him who conquers his enemies; for the hardest victory is the victory over self." — Aristotle

Power of Prayer

Prayer power seems able even to normalize the aging process, obviating or limiting infirmity and deterioration. You need not lose your basic energy or vital power or become weak and listless merely as a result of accumulating years. It is not necessary to allow your spirit to sag or grow stale or dull. Prayer can freshen you up every evening and send you out renewed each morning. You can receive guidance in problems if prayer is allowed to permeate your subconscious, the seat of the forces which determines whether you take right or wrong actions. Prayer has the power to keep your reactions correct and sound. Prayer driven deeply into your subconscious can remake you. It releases and keeps power flowing freely.

People are doing more praying today than formerly because they find that it adds to personal efficiency. Prayer helps them to tap forces and to utilize strength not otherwise available. A famous psychologist says, "Prayer is the greatest power available to the individual in solving his personal problems. Its power astonishes me." Prayer power is a manifestation of energy. Just as there exist scientific techniques for the release of atomic energy, so are there scientific procedures for the release of spiritual energy through the mechanism of prayer. Exciting demonstrations of this energizing force are evident. If you have not experienced this power, perhaps you need to learn new techniques of prayer.

Lord Osho

Osho is known as the most revolutionary preacher in the world.
His real name was Chandra Mohan Jain and pet name Rajneesh.
He was named Osho because of his knowledge like an ocean.
Osho was born in 1931 at Raisen, Madhya Pradesh, India.
He did M.A in philosophy and worked for a newspaper.
He was appointed as the professor of philosophy in Jabalpur.
As an atheist, he took interest RSS, Indian Army, and hypnosis.
He had conflicts with lecturers and considered dangerous for students.
He tore out all certificates, abandoned teaching, and travelled India.
He began public speaking at annual Sarva Dharma Sammelan at Jabalpur.
Osho criticized socialism, Gandhi, and religion that made him controversial.
Osho began meditation camps and spoke openly about physical union.
First he initiated a group in Mumbai and then shifted to Pune.
He travelled to the USA and criticized openly about Christianity.
President Reagan and 21 other countries prohibited Osho's entrance.
He returned to Pune and died in 1990 after heart failure.

"If learning hasn't changed your behaviour, then it means it didn't come in you." – Indira Gandhi

It is important to choose the right affirmation for the specific situation. You also need to feel comfortable with the words you repeat, so as not to awaken inner resistance. Affirmations can be used together with creative visualization, to strengthen it, and they can be used separately, on their own. They are of special importance for people who find it difficult to visualize, and can serve as a substitute to creative visualization.

Instead of repeating negative and useless words and phrases in the mind, choose positive words and phrases to help you build the life you want. By choosing your thoughts and words you exercise control over your life. Here are a few affirmations:

- ❖ Day by day I am becoming happier and more satisfied.
- ❖ With every inhalation, I am filling myself with happiness.
- ❖ Love is now filling my life.
- ❖ The power of the Cosmos is filling my life with love.
- ❖ My relationships with… are improving.
- ❖ I have now a wonderful job, which pays well.
- ❖ A lot of money is flowing now into my life.
- ❖ The power of the Universal Mind is now filling my life with wealth.
- ❖ The powerful, and vital energy of the Cosmos, is flowing and filling my body and mind.
- ❖ Healing energy is constantly filling every cell of my body.
- ❖ I always stay calm and in control of myself, in every situation and in all circumstances.
- ❖ I am having a wonderful, happy and fascinating day.

"Some people would compromise in small things if they weren't troubled with great ambition."
– Ludwig Wittgenstein

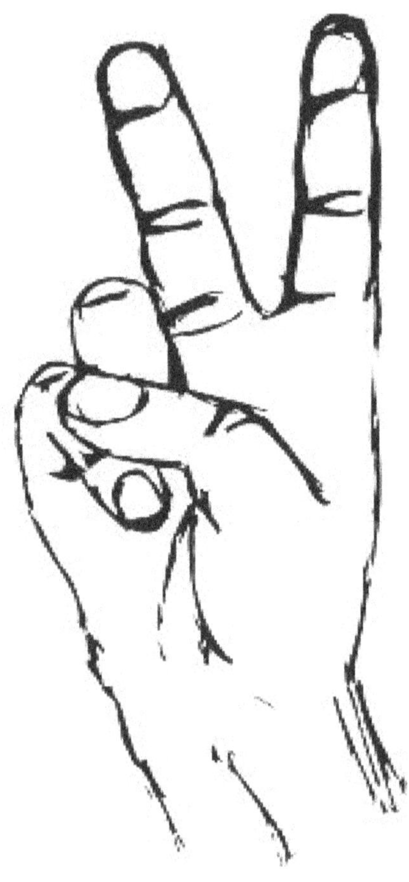

"Reading is the sublime engagement of people with optimism." – Niranjan Jha Showman

"You can't become who you want to be if you are too attached to who you have been." – Socrates

"Let good grow against bad because the growth of bad is perilous." – Niranjan Jha Showman

"Live as if you were to die tomorrow and learn as if you were to live forever." – Mahatma Gandhi

"A fool finds wisdom in his own delirium." – Niranjan Jha Showman

"Educating the mind without educating the heart is no education at all." – Aristotle

"A country elects a thief when it feels its success is in thievery." – Niranjan Jha Showman

"There is a difference between reading to know and reading to learn." – Niranjan Jha Showman

"The biggest undeveloped area of the world is underneath your cap." – Lewis Carroll

"The habit of listening to lies destroys the ability of understanding truth." – Niranjan Jha Showman

"Donating to poor is easy, the important is to not allow poverty to arise." – Niranjan Jha Showman

"The hardest decision is whether to walk away or try harder." – Graham Bell

"Where all else lose courage, a history maker begins from." – Niranjan Jha Showman

"Winning is joyful but striving to win is also not less." – Niranjan Jha Showman

"The problem is not the problem but your attitude about the problem." – Johnny Depp

"True learning never happens without pain." – Niranjan Jha Showman

"No problem can be solved from the same level of consciousness that created it." – Einstein

"Too much of political lies kills a nation." – Niranjan Jha Showman

"People, instead of trying to be good are looking for good persons." – Gloria Stenum

"Sinking too much in poverty will make you hate riches." – Niranjan Jha Showman

"The man who does more than he is paid for will sooner be paid for more than he does." – Napoleon Hill

"You can't become who you want to be if you are too attached to who you have been." – Socrates

"Victory is not the property of brilliants but the crown of those who work hard confidently." – Bonaparte

"When the going gets tough, the tough gets going." – Proverb

"There are two kind of people on earth: who is he, and who is who." – Daniel H. Pink

"If you laugh the world laughs with you, if you cry the world still laughs." – Proverb

"Talents means first having a great courage to bear troubles." – Carlice

"Don't compare yourself with anyone, if you do so, you are insulting yourself." – Alen Strike

"Men don't live for bread only but confidence, sympathy and appreciation also." – Emerson

"It is hard to believe in God, but it is harder to live without God."- Rousseau

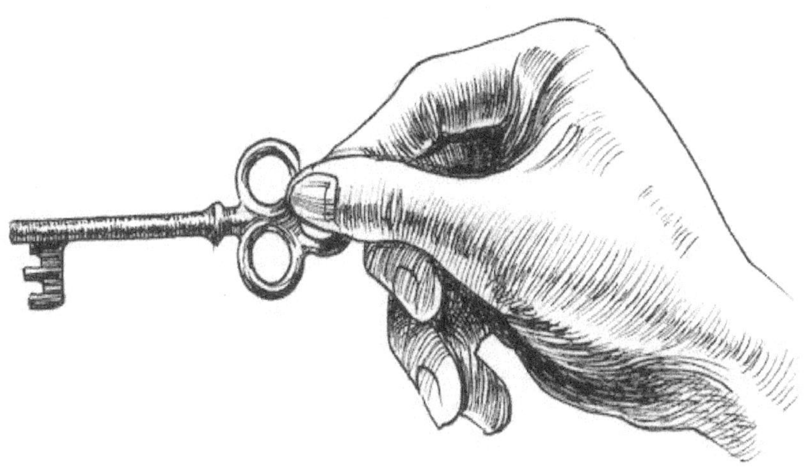

"It is bad to fail but it is even worse not to have tried to succeed." – Swett Marden

"The work of today becomes the destiny of tomorrow." – Plato

"When something is on stake, only then a person tries his best." – Abdul Kalam

"The greatest glory in living lies not in never falling, but in rising every time we fall." – Nelson Mandela

"Education is the ability to meet life's situation." – Dale Carnegie

"If you are not willing to risk unusual, you will have to settle for the ordinary." – Jim Rohn

"Learning without thought is labour lost; thought without learning is perilous." – Confucius

"You can't dream yourself into a character; you must hammer and forge yourself." - Swett Marden

"The way to get started is to quit talking and begin doing." – Walt Disney

"Giving a fish removes the hunger of a day. Teaching fishing removes the hunger of the entire life." – Confucius

"Millions said the apple fell but Newton was the one to ask why." – Baruch

"If you open a school, it closes one hundred jails." – Proverb

"Everyone thinks of changing the world, no one thinks of changing himself." – Leo Tolstoy

"Our truest life is when we are in our dreams awake." – Henry Thoreau

"Work saves us from three evils: boredom, vice and needs." – Voltaire

"Men are not born by circumstances but create them." – Rousseau

"When you burn your finger, you always blame the fire." – Proverb

"Glory consists not in never falling, but rising every time we fall." – Confucius

"Education is the chief defence of nation." – Edmund Burke

"Study is needful to mind as exercise for body." – Joseph Addison

"The more curious we are, the more creative we become." – Barbara Cartland

"A journey of thousand miles begins with a single step." – Vivekanand

"The man with imagination is never alone." – Bible

"A real talented person cannot live without doing what he can." – Abdul Kalam

"The cause of human development is curiosity." – Newton

"The value of life is dedication for a great goal." – Graham Bell

"Beauty is in the eyes of beholder." – Shakespeare

"Prove all things but hold fast which is better." – Bhagavad Gita

"Too high standard obstruct progress." – Lincoln

"Don't do with others what you don't like with yourself." – Quran

"Throw an intelligent man into water and he will come up with a crocodile." – Proverb

"Only men get born crying, live complaining, and die worrying." – Swett Marden

"Don't put off till tomorrow what you can do today." – Proverb

"Men are willing to believe what they wish." – Harold Robbins

"A river cannot sing until it has rocks in its bottom." – Proverb

"The tragedy of life doesn't lie in not reaching your goal, but having no goal to reach." – Mays

"A sleeping fox catches no poultry." – Proverb

"Language is the dress of thought." – Swett Marden

"One who wants to please all, please none." – Proverb

"Freedom without discipline leads to destruction." – Napoleon Hill

"Ability breeds success but character keeps it alive." – Dale Carnegie

"The wastage of time is half suicide." – Proverb

"One who catches fish must not mind getting wet." – Proverb

"Corrupt time is tough for honest and honest time is tough for corrupt." – Shiv Khera

"Nothing happens until it is made to happen." – Proverb

"It takes both rain and sunshine to create a rainbow." – Proverb

"Did but never thought, thought but never did: both are stupid." – Osho

"A hammer shatters glass but forges steel." – Proverb

"A quitter never wins and a winner never quits." – Napoleon Hill

"Every crackpot is waiting for a jackpot." – Shiv Khera

"Every unfailure person is not successful." – Shiv Khera

"To activate mind is the aim of all educations." – Proverb

"If you have never made a mistake, you may have never tried a new thing." – Einstein

"Until you think which of the two books you should read, your neighbour reads both." – Swett Marden

When time is good, people say that they don't need to do anything else, and when time is bad, they say that they can't do anything. Happiness comes in life by doing good work, and you do good work when you are happy. You can teach a student a lesson for a day; but if you can teach him to learn by creating curiosity, he will continue the learning as long as he lives. No matter how much your forebears have struggled to bring you into a new world, you have to do your own struggle to avert darkness. The world is not willing to welcome those who find problems only, it needs those who find solutions. Most of the buildings of success are founded upon the pillar of sacrifices.

– Niranjan Jha Showman

....

Cromosys Publication

Be Millionaire Like Me

Niranjan Jha Showman

NIRANJAN JHA SHOWMAN

Founder - Niranjan Jha Showman

Education and Technology Research Center

Patankar Park, Nallasopara (W), Mumbai. +91-9561450045

Education, Technology, Publication, Healthcare, Newsmedia, Realtor, Filmmaking

www.facebook.com/cromosys

Cromosys Publication
Teach
Yourself
German
NIRANJAN JHA SHOWMAN

Cromosys Publication
Teach
Yourself
French
NIRANJAN JHA SHOWMAN

Cromosys Publication
Teach
Yourself
Spanish
NIRANJAN JHA SHOWMAN

Cromosys Publication

English
Voice
Accent and
Pronunciation

NIRANJAN JHA SHOWMAN

Teach Yourself Autodesk MAYA

Cromosys Publication

NIRANJAN JHA SHOWMAN

Cromosys Publication
Teach
Yourself
Autodesk
3ds Max
NIRANJAN JHA SHOWMAN

Cromosys Publication
CRIMINAL FACTORY
NIRANJAN JHA SHOWMAN

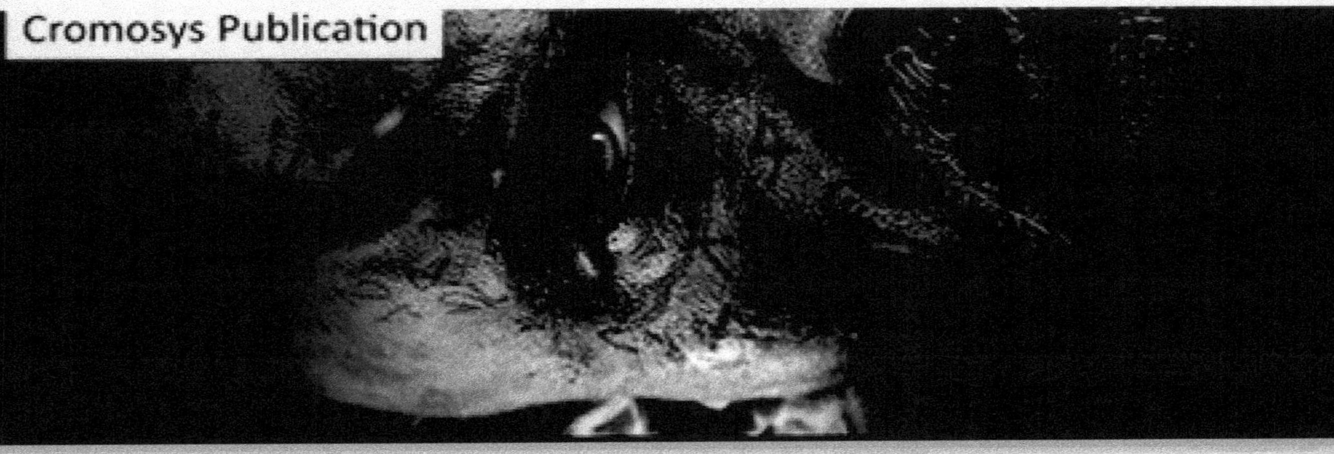

NIRANJAN JHA SHOWMAN
FOCAL DISASTER
Cromosys Publication

Cromosys Publication
Your talents will not help you succeed
without your skill of using them.
NIRANJAN JHA SHOWMAN
BE
MILLIONAIRE
LIKE
ME

Copyright Office
Government of India

सत्यमेव जयते

Extracts
from the Register
of Copyrights

Dated : 17/08/2022

1.	Registration Number	:	**T-98682-2022**
2.	Name, address and nationality of the applicant	:	NIRANJAN JHA SHOWMAN, CROMOSYS PUBLICATION, 001, JAYSATYAM, PATANKAR ROAD, NALLASOPARA (W), MUMBAI MAHARASHTRA - 401203. INDIAN
3.	Nature of the applicant's interest in the copyright of the work	:	AUTHOR
4.	Class and description of the work	:	LITERARY / BOOK
5.	Title of the work	:	**Be Millionaire Like me**
6.	Language of the work	:	ENGLISH
7.	Name, address and nationality of the author and if the author is deceased, date of his decease	:	NIRANJAN JHA SHOWMAN, CROMOSYS PUBLICATION, 001, JAYSATYAM, PATANKAR ROAD, NALLASOPARA (W), MUMBAI MAHARASHTRA - 401203. INDIAN
8.	Whether the work is published or unpublished	:	UNPUBLISHED
9.	Year and country of first publication and name, address and nationality of the publisher	:	N.A.
10.	Years and countries of subsequent publications, if any, and names, addresses and nationalities of the publishers	:	N.A. SAME AS ABOVE
11.	Names, addresses and nationalities of the owners of various rights comprising the copyright in the work and the extent of rights held by each, together with particulars of assignments and licences, if any	:	
12.	Names, addresses and nationalities of other persons, if any, authorised to assign or licence of rights comprising the copyright	:	N.A.
13.	If the work is an 'Artistic work', the location of the original work, including name, address and nationality of the person in possession of the work. (In the case of an architectural work, the year of completion of the work should also be shown).	:	N.A.
14.	If the work is an 'Artistic work', whether it is registered under the Designs Act 2000 if yes give details.	:	N.A.
15.	If the work is an 'Artistic work', capable of being registered as a design under the Designs Act 2000.whether it has been applied to an article though an industrial process and ,if yes ,the number of times it is reproduced.	:	N.A.
16.	Remarks, if any	:	

Diary Number :   9763/2020-DF/T
Date of Application :   25/07/2021
Date of Receipt :   25/07/2021

DEPUTY REGISTRAR OF COPYRIGHTS